SELECTED POEMS

WILLIAM DUNBAR was probably born in 1461 in the Lothians in the south-east of Scotland. He studied at St Andrews University, receiving the degree of MA in 1479. He later took holy orders and was ordained a priest in 1504, by which time he was employed in a clerical capacity at the court of James IV. He was part of the embassy which was sent to the English court in 1501 to negotiate the marriage contract between James IV and Margaret Tudor, and continued in royal employment until 1513, when he vanishes from sight after the battle of Flodden. It is not known whether he died in the battle or lived on in obscurity after it.

HARRIET HARVEY WOOD read English and Mediaeval Studies at Edinburgh University. She joined the British Council in 1973, becoming its Literature Director, a post which she held until her retirement in 1994. She is currently working on a biography of John Gibson Lockhart and (with A.S. Byatt) on an anthology on memory. She was a judge of the Booker Prize for Fiction in 1992 and is now a member of its Advisory Committee. She was appointed OBE in 1993.

Fyfield*Books* aim to make available some of the great classics of British and European literature in clear, affordable formats, and to restore often neglected writers to their place in literary tradition.

Fyfield*Books* take their name from the Fyfield elm in Matthew Arnold's 'Scholar Gypsy' and 'Thyrsis'. The tree stood not far from the village where the series was originally devised in 1971.

> *Roam on! The light we sought is shining still.*
> *Dost thou ask proof? Our tree yet crowns the hill,*
> *Our Scholar travels yet the loved hill-side*

from 'Thyrsis'

WILLIAM DUNBAR

Selected Poems

Edited with an introduction by
HARRIET HARVEY WOOD

Fyfield*Books*

CARCANET

To my Mother
Nor latt no wyld weid full of churlicheness
Compair hir till the lilleis nobilness

First published in Great Britain in 1999 by
Carcanet Press Limited
Alliance House
Cross Street
Manchester M2 7AQ

This impression 2003

A CIP catalogue record for this book is available from the British Library
ISBN 1 85754 719 5

The publisher acknowledges financial assistance from Arts Council England

Printed and bound in England by SRP Ltd, Exeter

CONTENTS

INTRODUCTION

In studying Dunbar, it is necessary to start with some negatives: we do not know when he was born, we do not know when he died; we know very little about the facts of his life and we do not know how many contemporary references to a William Dunbar (since it was a fairly common name) are in fact to the poet. Over eighty poems are attributed to him with varying degrees of authority, but we have no idea how much more of his work has been lost; reference to his own list of recently-deceased Scottish poets in the 'Lament for the Makaris' reminds us how little we know of the work of most of them and how much of the context in which Dunbar himself worked has disappeared. We do not know when most of his poems were written. It follows, therefore, that any attempt at a biographical sketch must be largely hypothetical, and that the information on which it is based must be drawn in the main from unreliable or at least unverifiable sources. The only firm facts about his career come from the accounts of the Lord High Treasurer for Scotland,[1] where various grants made to him are recorded. The rest is conjecture.

For his birth, the only evidence we have is Kennedy's allegation in the *Flyting*[2] that he was conceived 'in the gret eclips'. This has been assumed to refer to the total eclipse of the sun on 18 July 1460, which would put his birth in that year or 1461. It has been pointed out[3] that the eclipse could not have been seen in Scotland, nor indeed anywhere else north-west of Italy, and this fact has been held to discredit still further any biographical information which might be gleaned from so unreliable a source as a flyting. To quote Tom Scott, 'Nothing certain can be deduced from his flyting with Kennedy, because the convention of lies, exaggeration, abuse, scurrility, forbid one's treating such a source as reliable'.[4] Apart from the fact that some information in the *Flyting*

1   *Accounts of the Lord High Treasurer of Scotland, 1473–1538*, eds T. Dickson and J. Balfour Paul (6 vols, 1877–1905), quoted in future as *LHTA*.
2   No. 7 in this volume
3   Denton Fox, *PQ*, xxxix (1960), 414–15
4   Scott, p.2

is known to be accurate (for example, the fact that Dunbar was a priest), this overlooks a point which should be taken into consideration, namely, that the exaggeration and abuse in the *Flyting* loses its point if it is not founded on at least a grain of truth. When Kennedy says that Dunbar was priested by Satan, the remark gains point from the fact that Dunbar *was* a priest. Similarly, when he describes Dunbar as an 'yrle' or 'dearch' (dwarf), we do not necessarily take it literally, but the jibe would not have amused the audience if he had been a man of average or above-average height. We are therefore entitled in the absence of other evidence to assume that he was probably on the short side, possibly shorter than Kennedy. This receives purely impressionistic support from the charming picture of Dunbar capering in the dance in the queen's chamber:[5] this is not evidence but it conveys, somehow, the image of a small man.

The visibility of the eclipse in Scotland also seems less than conclusive. Granted that no one in north-west Europe could have seen it, the fact that Kennedy mentions it indicates that he and (it must be presumed) his audience all knew about it and when it took place. Few people in Britain, after all, actually saw Halley's Comet on its last visitation, but most of them knew about it and many will remember when it happened. For astronomically-minded people (and most educated men in the Middle Ages were astronomically-minded), the eclipse would have been a spectacular and significant event, and the fact of having been conceived during it is the kind of thing which a man might boast of, and his friends remember – and twist into an uncomplimentary reference in a flyting.

Since it is likely from other evidence that Dunbar was born within five years either side of 1460, it is probably not enormously important whether Kennedy's jibe was based on fact or not. The hypothetical date of 1460–61 is supported by the appearance of a William Dunbar in the St Andrews University records on dates which would fit well with this birth date. This William Dunbar was a determinant (that is, B.A.) of the University in 1477, and since the minimum age for this was sixteen, it is perfectly plausible to suppose that he may have been the poet. If so, he was not a poor scholar; he was able to pay his university fees, the infer-

5   No. 19 below

ence being that he had family behind him. The further record of the degree of Licentiate (or M.A.) was conferred on this Dunbar in 1479, and entitled him to teach, which fits with the fact that our Dunbar is commonly referred to as 'Maister'. If he is not the graduate of St Andrews, he must have gained a Master's degree somewhere else. But it would add further wit to the opening of his plea to the King, 'Sanct Salvatour! send silver sorrow' if he were known to be a graduate of the college of St Salvator in St Andrews.

After that, there is a gap until August 1500, when he was awarded a yearly pension of £10 (to end if he received a benefice of more than £40 per annum). Kennedy, in the *Flyting*, accuses Dunbar of having scuppered a voyage of the *Katryne*, so that he had to be landed on the Bass Rock. It has been assumed that this was a voyage made to France and other countries by Lord Bothwell on this ship to seek a bride for James IV. Bothwell left Scotland in May 1491 and returned without a bride, and only the *Flyting* suggests that Dunbar was with him; there is, however, a reference by Dunbar himself in the *Flyting* to a sea voyage in which the ship on which he was travelling was blown off course 'by Holland, Seland, ʒetland, and Northway coist', and it is conjectured that this may have been the mission of Sir James Ogilvie of Airlie to Denmark in 1492 to negotiate a treaty on behalf of James IV. One way or another, it seems safe to assume that during this blank period, Dunbar was involved in a long voyage with some kind of diplomatic mission, an assumption which is to some extent confirmed by the fact that he was employed on the embassy which was sent to London in October 1501 to negotiate the king's marriage contract with Margaret Tudor. On 31 December, it is recorded that King Henry VII gave £6.13s.4d to 'the Rhymer of Scotland in rewarde', and some time between December 1501 and May 1502 the payment of his pension in Scotland is annotated 'efter he com furth of Ingland'. It has been conjectured that Henry VII's payment was 'in rewarde' for the composition of 'London thow art of Townys A per se', the story running that 'in the Cristmas weke the mair had to dyner the Ambassadours of Scotland whome accompanyed my lord Chaunceler and other lordis of this Realme where sitting at dyner one of the said Scottis givying attendaunce upon a Bisshop ambassadour the which was Reported to be a prothnotary of Scotland and servaunt of the said Bisshop made this Balade folowying'.[6] The ambiguity of dates, the fact that Andrew Forman, not Dunbar, was pronotary on this expedition and the English spelling of the text of the poem (though this could easily be attributed to English scribes) have prevented this poem from being universally accepted as part of Dunbar's canon; but there seems little doubt that he was in England at that time, and the poem may well be his.

Further doubt obscures his ecclesiastical career. We know that he was ordained, since James IV made an offering of seven French crowns for his first mass (a common custom at the time) on 17 March 1504. If he was indeed part of Lord Bothwell's mission which sailed on the *Katryne*, it implies that by 1491 he was employed, presumably in some clerical capacity, at court. What had he done in the twelve years or so since he graduated? He says himself in 'How Dumbar was desyred to be ane Freir'[7] that

> Gif evir my fortoun wes to be a freir
> The dait thairof is past fully mony a ȝeir;
> For into every lusty toun and place
> Off all Yngland, frome Berwick to Kalice,
> I haif in to thy habeit maid gud cheir.
>
> In freiris weid full fairly haif I fleichit;
> In it haif I in pulpet gon and preichit
> In Derntoun kirk and eik in Canterberry;
> In it I past at Dover our the ferry
> Throw Piccardy, and thair the peple teichit.

and this gains some corroboration from Kennedy's allegation that

> Fra Etrike Forest furthward to Drumfrese
> Thou beggit wyth a pardoun in all kirkis.[8]

The picture that emerges is that of a man of a reasonably well-to-do East Lothian family (he refers to himself as from Lothian in the *Flyting*) who could afford to support him at university (the records show that he was not a poor scholar, his fees were paid),

6   British Library, MS Cotton Vitellius A xvi, ff. 199b–200. The poem is also found in Lansdowne MS 762, f. 7b and Balliol College MS394, where it is described as 'a litill balet made by london made at mr shawes [Sir John Shaw, Lord Mayor] table by a skote'.
7   No. 4 below
8   No. 7, ll.425–26

possibly illegitimate but acknowledged, but if legitimate, probably a younger son who would have to make his own way in the world. He had no inheritance in the only thing that then mattered, land. For an intelligent young man in such a situation, the church was the obvious choice of career, and Dunbar implies that he was indeed bred for it:

> I wes in 30uthe on nureice kne
> Cald dandillie, bischop, dandillie.[9]

Success in such a career would depend very much on family influence, and Dunbar's lack of success in gaining the kind of preferment his fellow-poet, Gavin Douglas, Bishop of Dunkeld, achieved, argues that his family lacked the necessary influence. In the pursuit of such a career, it is not implausible that he might have spent some years after university seeing the world as a Franciscan novice (James IV was particularly well disposed to the Friars Observant Franciscans and made regular retreats to their Stirling house, but there was also an important community in Edinburgh) before being employed at court as some sort of secretary or official. The precise nature of his employment is unlikely ever to be known, but he is described on one document on which he appears as witness as 'chaplain' and it is likely that his duties were both secretarial and religious. The £10 a year pension he was awarded in 1500 was probably for such services rather than for his poems, since the king was notoriously ungenerous to men of letters. He himself admits that 'Allace, I can bot ballatis breif' in one of his pleas to the king (no. 15, 1.48) which makes it unlikely that he was employed administratively in any but a fairly junior capacity, but he makes it clear elsewhere that he set a high value on his ballads and might well consider them of more importance than any of his secretarial duties. Whether he would in fact have been contented, as he claimed, with 'ane kirk scant coverit with hadder [heather]'[10] is perhaps doubtful, and whether he ever got it is unknown. He vanishes from the records in 1513, the year of Flodden, and nothing more is known of him. His orders need not have prevented him from fighting (two bishops and two abbots died in action on the Scottish side) but at his age he was unlikely

---

9 No. 15, ll.61–2
10 'This wavering warldis wretchidness', l.86

to have borne arms. As one of the king's chaplains, he might have accompanied him to the battlefield and been killed in the rout. Or he might have got his little church thatched with heather and retired from court life. There is a poem of consolation addressed to the Queen Dowager in the Bannatyne MS which has been attributed to Dunbar and which, if his, must have been written in 1514 before her remarriage; and there is another, 'Quhen the Governour Past in Fraunce', ascribed to him in the Maitland Folio, which, if correctly attributed, would prove his survival to 1517, 1522 or 1524, in all of which years the Regent, the Duke of Albany, left Scotland for France.

The frequency of Dunbar's poetical begging letters to the king and complaints of his empty purse tend to obscure the fact that, though he might not have achieved a bishopric, he did not go entirely unrewarded. The pension of £80 a year and perks which he finally achieved in 1510 (to be paid until he received a benefice of £100 or more) made him, as Mackay Mackenzie points out, 'as well off as Chaucer on his final pension of £20, and latterly much better off than Hector Boece, whose stipend as Principal of King's College, Aberdeen, was … £26.13s.4d.'.[11] It is not to be doubted that at times he was genuinely hard up, that he was an ambitious man conscious of his own worth who felt that he deserved better; possibly he longed in theory for the independence of court which preferment would have given him, though one suspects that he would in fact have missed the life. His frequent complaints of the corrupt court atmosphere (probably well-founded), of those who 'standis in a nuk and rownes [whispers]'[12] obscure the fact that it was court and city life which fired his imagination and provided the stimulation for most of his poetry.

The court of James IV has gone down in legend as the golden age of medieval Scotland, and so in some respects it was, though the glories of its circumstances and achievements were to some extent comparative. For those who wish to explore its more negative aspects, Tom Scott[13] has provided an excellent description. Not the least of the achievements of James IV and his father in his

11 p. xxii. Baxter (p. 182) puts Boece's salary at £50 a year. Either way, Dunbar was doing much better.
12 'Aganis the Solistaris in Court', l.13
13 Dunbar, a critical exposition of the poems

later reign was to avert, by a prudent succession of truces, the constant threat of English invasion, though James IV's support of Perkin Warbeck pushed this dangerously far, and even this blessing came to an end with the ill-considered adventure of Flodden. It was certainly this period of peace which gave James the opportunity to extend his diplomacy and commerce much more widely throughout Europe than many of his predecessors had done and so gave Dunbar the opportunity to travel abroad on his missions. It also gave James the opportunity to cultivate peaceful and intellectual pursuits and there is ample evidence that he did so. The famous description of him by Pedro de Ayala, the ambassador sent to Scotland by Ferdinand and Isabella of Spain, may be exaggerated in some respects but is based on reality:

> He is of noble stature, neither tall nor short, and as handsome in complexion and shape as a man can be. His address is very agreeable. He speaks the following foreign languages: Latin, very well; French, German, Flemish, Italian, and Spanish... His own Scotch language is as different from English as Aragonese from Castilian. The king speaks, besides, the language of the savages who live in some parts of Scotland and on the islands... He is well read in the Bible and in some other devout books. He is a good historian. He has read many Latin and French histories, and profited by them, as he has a very good memory.

But he adds more ominously,

> He is courageous, even more so than a king should be. I am a good witness of it. I have seen him often undertake most dangerous things in the last wars. I sometimes clung to his skirts and succeeded in keeping him back. On such occasions he does not take the least care of himself. He is not a good captain, because he begins to fight before he has given his orders.[14]

This last characteristic was to be fatally exhibited at Flodden. And though the king's interest in and support of education, history, medicine, architecture, shipbuilding, printing, and other crafts

---

14   P. Hume Brown, *Early Travellers in Scotland* (Edinburgh, 1891), pp. 39–40.

(Dunbar provides a good list of them in no. 12) was creditable, he appears to have been less interested in literature – 'ab literis incultus', says George Buchanan. Dunbar had some genuine cause for complaint.

It says much for Dunbar's skill, however, that a poetic output in which complaints and begging poems play so large a part has contrived to retain its freshness and ingenuity five hundred years later. This has been ascribed to his versatility and virtuosity in metre, diction and form, but there is more to it than that. In Dunbar, more than in any other medieval poet, an individual personality appears. Whether he is bewailing his headache or complaining that an idiot has tampered maliciously with his poems, lamenting over his empty purse or dancing in the Queen's chamber till his slipper falls off, Dunbar himself is there before us, recognisable and completely unmistakeable. His greatest predecessor, Henryson, also leaves a picture of himself in his work but it is more diffused, less subjective. With Dunbar it is concentrated. He is essentially a performance poet, and his own personality was an important part of the performance. C.S. Lewis complains that we remain his audience, not his confidants, 'cut off from him (as it were) by the footlights'.[15] This seems not quite fair; if there are occasions when we do indeed confront him across the footlights – and one must remember that, however high Dunbar himself set the craft of poetry, he would undoubtedly have been seen by most of his patrons more as a court entertainer than anything else – there are certainly others where he takes the mask off: in no. 8, for instance, where the voice of a sad, depressed ageing man comes through in his dread of a Scottish winter:

> Quhone that the nycht dois lenthin houris
> With wind, with haill and havy schouris,
> My dule spreit dois lurk for schoir,
> My hairt for langour dois forloir
> For laik of Symmer with his flouris,

and, in one of the most effectively sinister lines,

> And than sayis Age, 'My freind, cum neir
> And be not strange...'

15   C.S. Lewis, *English Literature in the Sixteenth Century* (Oxford, 1968), p. 98

But the hopeful ending seems equally in character:

> 3it quhone the nycht begynnis to schort
> It dois my spreit sum pairt confort
> Off thocht oppressit with the schowris;
> Cum lustie Symmer with thi flowris,
> That I may leif in sum disport.

It is partly a misfortune for Dunbar that the sheer virtuosity and ingenuity of his work has to some extent obscured his own voice.

His ingenuity is indeed remarkable, the more so as he worked almost exclusively within established medieval conventions, many of them looking a little tired by the end of the fifteenth century. It would be too much to claim that he inspired new life into the garden of the Rose, though even there he contrives to inject some very Scottish realism into his reply to May when challenged, in no. 2, to arise and write something in her honour:

> Quhairto, quod I, sall I uprys at morrow
> For in this May few birdis herd I sing?
> Thai haif moir caus to weip and plane thair sorrow,
> Thy air it is nocht holsum nor benyng;
> Lord Eolus dois in thy sessone ring;
> So busteous ar the blastis of his horne,
> Amang they bewis to walk I haif forborne.

After this reasonable complaint of an Edinburgh spring, however, the dream proceeds on fairly conventional lines as he celebrates the union of James IV and Margaret Tudor, not forgetting as he does so to admonish the notoriously randy king to restrict his extra-marital amours in future. It ends with a trick which he was to use in many of his dream poems, with the poet being wakened by the loudness of the birds' singing; just as the pretend friar in no. 4 wakes him by vanishing 'with stynk and fyrie smowk', and the yammering and shrieking of the birds wakes him in no. 23, and the devil shitting on the tailor in no. 31 makes him laugh so much that it wakes him again. It is a trick which grows naturally out of the substance of the poem and never fails to anchor the dream to the real world.

But although he is often described as a Chaucerian, Dunbar was heir to more than one legacy; indeed, one of the remarkable features of his work is how easily and apparently effortlessly he contrived to harness different poetic traditions. A couple of stanzas from 'The Golden Targe' illustrates this process:

Doune throu the ryce a ryvir ran wyth stremys
So lustily agayn thai lykand lemys
That all the lake as lamp did leme of licht,
Quhilk schadowit all about wyth twynkling glemis
That bewis bathit war in secund bemys
Throu the reflex of Phebus visage brycht:
On every syde the hegies raise on hicht,
The bank was grene, the bruke was full of bremys,
The stanneris clere as stern in frosty nycht.

The cristall air, the sapher firmament,
The ruby skyes of the orient
Kest beriall bemes on emerant bewis grene;
The rosy garth depaynt and redolent
With purpur, azure, gold and goulis gent
Arayed was by dame Flora the quene
So nobily that joy was for to sene;
The roch agayn the rivir resplendent
As low enlumynit all the leves schene.

The setting here comes straight from the *Roman de la Rose*, the dream allegory set in the traditional *locus amoenus*, and it is described in a stanza form which is a variant on the French rime royal. As used by Chaucer and Henryson, it was a seven-line octosyllabic stanza, rhyming ababbcc; Dunbar's nine-line version[16] was also used by Douglas in his *Palice of Honour*. The vocabulary is the aureate vocabulary of the French *grands rhetoriqueurs*, a style derived essentially from Latin and used originally mainly for religious writing, but also for courtly writing. Dunbar is notoriously celebrated as the user of aureate diction, though in fact he uses it sparingly and in its fullest flowering only in poems like no. 34 where he would see such use as manifestly appropriate. But even in this extract, in which there is, as would be expected in the garden of the rose, a high degree of aureation, there are touches which moderate and illuminate the Latinate and heraldic vocabulary: for example, 'the stanneris [pebbles] clere as stern [stars] in frosty nycht'. This does not come from the traditional May garden setting, this is the kind of poetic observation that strikes home.

16   He uses the seven-line version elsewhere, for example in no. 2 below

But there are also other things to be noted. Dunbar inherited not only from the Romantic but also from the Teutonic tradition, which came down to him from Old English through poems such as *Piers Plowman* and *Gawain and the Green Knight* and was extensively used in fifteenth-century Scotland, and even here it shows. The Old English stressed line of verse, divided into two half-lines by a caesura and linked by alliteration (usually in either three or four words), with the stresses falling on the alliteration, is used by him in its fullest form only in no. 28, though elements of it appear in other poems, for example no. 7. In these stanzas, many lines have not only heavy alliteration ('Doune throu the *r*yce a *r*yvir *r*an wyth stremys / So *l*ustily agayn thai *l*ykand *l*emys / That all the *l*ake as *l*amp did *l*eme of *l*icht'), but even retain echoes of the caesura, so that the first of the lines quoted could be read as 'Doune throu the *r*yce   a *r*yvir *r*an with stremys', which is a perfectly acceptable alliterative line, with the stresses falling on the initial letter 'r' throughout. Tom Scott has shown how much of Dunbar's apparently syllabic verse can be found to have also elements of the older stressed system.[17] Only a very confident and accomplished metrist could have contrived to synthesise these two systems so apparently easily. No wonder he resented the mangling by Mure of his poems.[18]

His mastery of metre is also apparent in his use of the lyric stanzas which came to him through the troubadours of Provence. No poet, before or since, has made more brilliant or haunting use of refrains:

> Quhilk to considder is ane pane
>
> Exces of thocht dois me mischeiff
>
> Telȝouris and sowtaris, blist be ye!
>
> Renunce thy God and cum to me
>
> All erdly joy returnis in pane
>
> *Timor mortis conturbat me.*

And if his refrains haunt the memory insistently, his opening lines are no less unforgettable:

17 Op. cit., chap. XIV
18 See no. 5 below

Complane I wald, wist I quhome till

Done is a battel on the dragon blak

In secreit place this hindir nycht

Lucina schynning in silence of the nicht

Now fayre, fayrest off every fayre

Sanct Salvatour, send silver sorrow.

If the matter that comes between the opening line and the refrain is sometimes not what might have been anticipated from the opening, then that is Dunbar's peculiar gift, to subvert expectation and turn conventions on their heads.

It has been alleged as a criticism of Dunbar that his technique is masterly but that his matter is slight, too slight to justify the care lavished on it. It cannot be denied that he does not address the grand universal themes that are to be found in the work of Chaucer and Henryson. His reputation has suffered, too, from the fact that much of his most substantial surviving work (for it must always be remembered how much may have been lost), is of a type which modern taste finds less comprehensible than his original audience. In reading him, to quote C.S. Lewis, 'we must sever the modern association which connects extreme indecency with technical coarseness of form and with low social rank, and must think ourselves back into a world where great professional poets, for the entertainment of great lords and ladies, lavished their skill on humours now confined to the preparatory school or the barrack room'.[19] Huizinga has pointed out how crudeness, in literature as in customs, contrasts with an excessive formalism, bordering on prudery, in the later Middle Ages, and adds that 'we should ... picture to ourselves two layers of civilization superimposed, coexisting though contradictory. Side by side with the courtly style, of literary and rather recent origin, the primitive forms of erotic life kept all their force'. And he instances in proof 'an epithalamium of extreme indecency' dedicated by Deschamps to Antoine de Bourgogne, and a lascivious ballad made at the request of the lady of Burgundy and her attendants.[20]

19   Op. cit., p. 94
20   Huizinga, p. 97

If this was so at the courts of France and Burgundy, with which he was chiefly concerned, how much more so must this have been the case in Scotland. It is in this context that the modern reader has to consider poems like 'Madam, ʒour men said thai wald ryd' (not included here) and 'A Brash of Wowing' and parts of *The Tua Mariit Wemen and the Wedo* and, indeed, the scatological elements of the *Flyting* and 'The Sowtar and Tailʒouris War' and 'The Fenʒeit Freir of Tungland', on which Priscilla Bawcutt has some very interesting remarks.[21]

It must also be remembered that his genius is for the short poem, satire and the lyric (a literary form which, interestingly, barely existed in Scotland before he wrote, if at all); while Chaucer and Henryson went for the longer distance, he was a sprinter. The longest of his surviving poems (no. 27) runs to only 530 lines; few exceed 200 lines. There are, for modern taste, too many poems of complaint and supplication, witty and beautifully constructed though many of them are. There is also the problem that satire tends not to wear well. Even Swift's victims inspire little interest two hundred years later. But within these limits, his subjects are not trivial, and nor is the way he treats them. C.S. Lewis has summed him up best:

> He was a very great man; when you are in the mood for it, his poetry has a sweep and volume of sound and an assured virility which (while the mood lasts) makes most other poets seem a little faint and tentative and half-hearted. If you like half-tones and nuances you will not enjoy Dunbar; he will deafen you.[22]

It has been the common practice for editors of Dunbar to divide his poems into groups, as Bannatyne, who preserved most of them, had done in his great collection: religious poems, love poems, poems of court life, dream poems, moral poems. This seems to me unsatisfactory, if only because so many categories overlap, while the love poem category barely exists at all (to include *The Tua Mariit Wemen and the Wedo* in such a group indicates a certain desperation). Is 'The Passion of Christ' a religious poem or a dream poem? Is 'The Thrissel and the Rose' a dream poem or a court poem? Under what heading can one put a flyting?

21   Priscilla Bawcutt, *Dunbar the Makar* (Oxford, 1992), pp. 239–41
22   Op. cit., p. 98

It is unsatisfactory, too, to try to arrange them in date order, since so few are dateable. I have preferred therefore to arrange them rather more haphazardly, which is the way I suspect they were written. There is a certain satisfaction in following the horror and indecency of 'Fasternis Evin in Hell' with the serene resignation of 'All Erdly Joy Returnis in Pane', and this is not due just to the fact that the one takes place on Shrove Tuesday and the other on Ash Wednesday.

Textual Note

No holograph versions of Dunbar's poems have survived. The textual history of many of them is complicated and, for a fuller account of the problems than can be given here, the reader is referred to the most recent and most comprehensive edition by Priscilla Bawcutt,[23] to which I am happy to acknowledge extensive debts. The only versions known to have appeared in his lifetime are the handful of poems printed by Chepman and Myllar (C&M) *c.* 1508; since it is possible that their texts may have been overseen by Dunbar himself, they have the highest claim to be followed. The main manuscript collections in which the poems included in this selection are found are (the abbreviations by which they are referred to given in brackets):

the Asloan MS (A), a miscellany of verse and prose made in the reign of James V, ed. W.A. Craigie, STS, 2 vols, 1923–4;

the Bannatyne MS (B), the largest known collection of early Scottish poetry, compiled by an Edinburgh merchant, George Bannatyne 'in tyme of pest', c. 1568, ed. W. Tod Ritchie, STS, 4 vols, 1928–34;

the Maitland Folio MS (M), a poetry miscellany compiled by Sir Richard Maitland of Lethington , c. 1570, ed. W.A. Craigie, STS, 2 vols, 1919 and 1927;

the Reidpeth MS (R), a transcript of M made in 1622 before part of M was lost, and now the only source for several poems ascribed to Dunbar, Cambridge University Library, Moore LL.v.10.

23 *The Poems of William Dunbar*, 2 vols (Association for Scottish Literary Studies, Glasgow, 1998).

The source of each poem is indicated in the notes. Texts are presented as far as possible in conformity with modern usage in matters of capitalisation, punctuation, etcetera, and all manuscript contractions have been silently expanded. Letters which were interchangeable in medieval manuscript convention (for example, i/j, u/w/v) are given in their most familiar modern version. The letter thorn is given as 'th', and yogh (normally pronounced simply as 'y') as '3', but the Scottish spelling conventions of 'quh' (for 'wh') and 'sch' (for 'sh') have been retained, as is the plural form, '-is'. Capitalisation, indentation and punctuation are editorial.

REFERENCES AND ABBREVIATIONS

Baildon	H. Bellyse Baildon ed., *The Poems of William Dunbar*, Cambridge, 1907
Bawcutt	Priscilla Bawcutt, *Dunbar the Makar*, Oxford, 1992
Bawcutt (ed.)	*The Poems of William Dunbar*, ed. Priscilla Bawcutt, 2 vols, Association for Scottish Literary Studies, Glasgow, 1998
Baxter	J.W. Baxter, *William Dunbar: a biographical study*, Edinburgh, 1952
Chaucer	*The Works of Geoffrey Chaucer*, ed. F.N. Robinson, Oxford, 1933
Douglas	*The Poetical Works of Gavin Douglas*, ed. John Small, 4 vols, Edinburgh, 1874
Henryson	*The Poems and Fables of Robert Henryson*, ed. H. Harvey Wood, revised edition, Edinburgh, 1958
Huizinga	J. Huizinga, *The Waning of the Middle Ages*, London, 1952
Kinsley	James Kinsley ed., *The Poems of William Dunbar*, Oxford, 1979
Lewis	C.S. Lewis, *English Literature in the Sixteenth Century excluding drama*, Oxford, 1968
—	*The Discarded Image, an introduction to medieval and renaissance literature*, Cambridge, 1964
—	*The Allegory of Love*, Oxford, 1936
LHTA	*Accounts of the Lord High Treasurer of Scotland, 1473–1538*, ed. T. Dickson and J. Balfour Paul, 6 vols, Edinburgh, 1877–1905
Mackenzie	*The Poems of William Dunbar*, ed. W. Mackay Mackenzie, Edinburgh, 1932; revised by Bruce Dickins and reprinted, London, 1966
Mackie	R. L. Mackie, *King James IV of Scotland*, Edinburgh, 1958
Mâle	Emile Mâle, *The Gothic Image*, trans. Dora Nussey, London, 1913; quoted here from Fontana Library edition, 1961

Nicholson	Ranald Nicholson, *Scotland: the Later Middle Ages*, Edinburgh History of Scotland, vol. 2, Edinburgh, 1974
Roman de la Rose	Guillaume de Lorris and Jean de Meung, *Le Roman de la Rose*, ed. Francisque-Michel, 2 vols, Paris, 1864
Sarum	*The Sarum Missal*, ed. J. Wickham Legg, Oxford, 1916
Scott	Tom Scott, *Dunbar: a critical exposition of the poems*, Edinburgh, 1966
Simpson Ross	Ian Simpson Ross, *William Dunbar*, Leiden, 1981
Small	*The Poems of William Dunbar*, eds John Small and Æ.J.G. MacKay, STS, 3 vols, 1884–93
STS	Scottish Text Society
Villon	A. Longnon ed., *François Villon, Oeuvres*, Classiques Français du Moyen Age, Paris, 1932

To speik of science, craft or sapience,
Off vertew, morall cunnyng or doctrene,
Off jure, of wisdome or intelligence,
Off everie study, lair, or disciplene;
All is bot tynt or reddie for to tyne,   5
Not using it as it sould usit be,
The craift exerceing, considdering not the fyne:
A paralous seiknes is vane prosperite.

The curious probatioun logicall,
The eloquence of ornat rethorie,   10
The naturall science philosophicall,
The dirk apperance of astronomie,
The theologis sermoun, the fablis of poetrie,
Without gud lyfe all in the selfe dois de,
As Maii flouris dois in September dry;   15
A paralous lyfe is vane prosperite.

Quhairfoir, ȝe clarkis and grittest of constance,
Fullest of science and of knawlegeing,
To us be myrrouris on ȝour governance,
And in our darknes be lamps in schyning,   20
Or than in frustar is ȝour lang leirning;
Giff to ȝour sawis your deidis contrair be,
ȝour maist accusar salbe ȝour awin cunning:
A paralus seiknes is vane prosperitie.

---

4 *lair*, learning   5 *tynt, tyne*, lost, lose   7 *fyne*, end   9 *curious*, subtle;
probatioun, proof   21 *in frustar*, in vain   22 *sawis*, sayings

2. THE THRISSIL AND THE ROIS

Quhen Merche wes with variand windis past,
And Appryll had, with hir silver schouris,
Tane leif at nature with ane orient blast,
And lusty May that muddir is of flouris
Had maid the birdis to begyn thair houris   5
Amang the tendir odouris reid and quhyt,
Quhois armony to heir it wes delyt,

In bed at morrow, sleiping as I lay,
Me thocht Aurora, with hir cristall ene
In at the window lukit by the day,   10
And halsit me, with visage paill and grene;
On quhois hand a lark sang fro the splene,
'Awalk, luvaris, out of ʒour slomering,
Se how the lusty morrow dois up spring'.

Me thocht fresche May befoir my bed upstude   15
In weid depaynt of mony divers hew,
Sobir, benyng, and full of mansuetude,
In brycht atteir of flouris forgit new,
Hevinly of color, quhyt, reid, broun and blew,
Balmit in dew and gilt with Phebus bemys   20
Quhill all the hous illumynit of hir lemys.

'Slugird' scho said, 'awalk annone for schame
And in my honour sum thing thow go wryt;
The lork hes done the mirry day proclame,
To rais up luvaris with confort and delyt,   25
ʒit nocht incress thy curage to indyt
Quhois hairt sum tyme hes glaid and blisfull bene,
Sangis to mak under the levis grene.'

---

8 *morrow*, morning   11 *halsit*, greeted   12 *splene*, heart   16 *weid*, garments
17 *mansuetude*, mildness   21 *lemys*, rays

'Quhairto,' quod I, 'sall I uprys at morrow
For in this May few birdis herd I sing?   30
Thai haif moir caus to weip and plane thair sorrow,
Thy air it is nocht holsum nor benyng;
Lord Eolus dois in thy sessone ring;
So busteous ar the blastis of his horne,
Amang thy bewis to walk I haif forborne.'   35

With that this lady sobirly did smyll
And said 'Uprys, and do thy observance;
Thow did promyt, in Mayis lusty quhyle,
For to discryve the ros of most plesance.
Go se the birdis how thay sing and dance,   40
Illumynit our with orient skyis brycht,
Annamyllit richely with new asur lycht.'

Quhen this wes said, depairtit scho, this quene,
And enterit in a lusty gairding gent;
And than, me thocht, full hestely besene,   45
In serk and mantill eftir hir I went
In to this garth, most dulce and redolent
Off herb and flour and tendir plantis sueit,
And grene levis doing of dew doun fleit.

The purpour sone, with tendir bemys reid,   50
In orient bricht as angell did appeir,
Throw goldin skyis putting up his heid,
Quhois gilt tressis schone so wondir cleir,
That all the world tuke confort, fer and neir,
To luke upone his fresche and blisfull face,   55
Doing all sable fro the hevynnis chace.

33 *sessone*, season; *ring*, reign   35 *bewis*, boughs   41 *our*, over   44 *gent*,
lovely   45 *besene*, arrayed   46 *serk*, shirt   47 *garth*, garden

3

And as the blisfull sonne of cherarchy
The fowlis song throw confort of the licht;
The birdis did with oppin vocis cry,
'O, luvaris fo, away thow dully nycht,   60
And welcum day that confortis every wicht;
Haill May, haill Flora, haill Aurora schene,
Haill princes Natur, haill Venus luvis quene'.

Dame Nature gaif ane inhibitioun thair
To fers Neptunus and Eolus the bawld   65
Nocht to perturb the wattir nor the air,
And that no schouris, nor blastis cawld,
Effray suld flouris nor fowlis on the fold;
Scho bad eik Juno, goddes of the sky,
That scho the hevin suld keip amene and dry.   70

Scho ordand eik that every bird and beist
Befoir hir hienes suld annone compeir,
And every flour of vertew, most and leist,
And every herb be feild fer and neir,
As thay had wont in May, fro ȝeir to ȝeir,   75
To hir thair makar to mak obediens,
Full law inclynnand with all dew reverens.

With that annone scho send the swyft ro
To bring in beistis of all conditioun;
The restles swallow commandit scho also   80
To feche all fowll of small and greit renown;
And, to gar flouris compeir of all fassoun,
Full craftely conjurit scho the ȝarrow,
Quhilk did furth swirk als swift as ony arrow.

57 *cherarchy*, heavenly host   68 *effray*, frighten   70 *amene*, pleasant   72
compeir, present themselves   83 *ȝarrow*, milfoil

4

All present wer in twynkling of ane E,   85
Baith beist and bird and flour befoir the quene,
And first the lyone, gretast of degre,
Was callit thair and he, most fair to sene,
With a full hardy contenance and kene,
Befoir dame Natur come, and did inclyne   90
With visage bawld and curage leonyne.

This awfull beist full terrible wes of cheir,
Persing of luke, and stout of countenance,
Rycht strong of corpis, of fassoun fair but feir,
Lusty of schaip, lycht of deliverance,   95
Reid of his cullour as is the ruby glance;
On feild of gold he stude full mychtely,
With flour delycis sirculit lustely.

This lady liftit up his cluvis cleir,
And leit him listly lene upone hir kne,   100
And crownit him with dyademe full deir
Off radyous stonis, most ryall for to se;
Saying, 'the King of Beistis mak I the,
And the cheif protector in woddis and schawis;
Onto thi leigis go furth, and keip the lawis.   105

Exerce Justice with mercy and conscience,
And lat no small beist suffir skaith na skornis
Of greit beistis that bene of moir piscence;
Do law elyk to aipis and unicornis,
And lat no bowgle, with his busteous hornis,   110
The meik pluch ox oppress, for all his pryd,
Bot in the 3ok go peciable him besyd.'

---

93 *stout*, brave   94 *but feir*, without equal   99 *cluvis*, claws   100 *listly*, easily
104 *schawis*, woods   107 *skaith*, harm   108 *piscence*, power   109 *elyk*, alike
110 *bowgle*, wild ox

Quhen this was said, with noyis and soun of joy,
All kynd of beistis in to thair degre
At onis cryit lawd, 'Vive le Roy!'   115
And till his feit fell with humilite,
And all thay maid him homege and fewte;
And he did thame ressaif with princely laitis,
Quhois noble yre is *parcere prostratis.*

Syne crownit scho the egle King of Fowlis,   120
And as steill dertis scherpit scho his pennis,
And bawd him be als just to awppis and owlis,
As unto pacokkis, papingais or crennis,
And mak a law for wycht fowlis and for wrennis;
And lat no fowll of ravyne do efferay,   125
Nor devoir birdis bot his awin pray.

Than callit scho all flouris that grew on feild,
Discirnyng all thair fassionis and effeiris;
Upon the awfull thrissill scho beheld
And saw him kepit with a busche of speiris;   130
Concedring him so able for the weiris,
A radius croun of rubeis scho him gaif,
And said, 'In feild go furth, and fend the laif;

And, sen thow art a king, thow be discreit;
Herb without vertew thow hald nocht of sic pryce   135
As herb of vertew and of odor sueit;
And lat no nettill vyle and full of vyce
Hir fallow to the gudly flour delyce;
Nor latt no wyld weid, full of churlichenes,
Compair hir till the lilleis nobilnes.   140

117 *fewte,* fealty   118 *laitis,* manners   121 *pennis,* feathers   123 *pacokkis,*
papingais or crennis, peacocks, parrots or cranes   124 *wycht,* strong   125 *do*
efferay, cause terror   128 *effeir,* behaviour   130 *kepit,* guarded   133 fend,
defend; *laif,* rest   138 *flour delyce,* heraldic lily

6

Nor hald non udir flour in sic denty
As the fresche ros of cullour reid and quhyt;
For gife thow dois, hurt is thyne honesty,
Conciddering that no flour is so perfyt,
So full of vertew, plesans and delyt,   145
So full of blisfull angeilik bewty,
Imperiall birth, honour and dignite.'

Than to the Ros scho turnyt hir visage
And said, 'O lusty dochtir most benyng,
Aboif the lilly, illustare of lynnage,   150
Fro the stok ryell rysing fresche and ȝing,
But ony spot or macull doing spring;
Cum blowme of joy with jemis to be cround,
For our the laif thy bewty is renownd.'

A coistly croun, with clarefeid stonis brycht,   155
This cumly quene did on hir heid inclois,
Quhill all the land illumynit of the licht;
Quhairfoir me thocht all flouris did rejos,
Crying attonis, 'Haill be thow richest Ros!
Haill, hairbis empryce, haill, freschest quene of flouris,   160
To the be glory and honour at all houris.'

Thane all the birdis song with voce on hicht,
Quhois mirthfull soun wes mervelus to heir;
The mavys song, 'Haill, Rois most riche and richt,
That dois up flureis undir Phebus speir;   165
Haill plant of ȝowth, haill princes dochtir deir,
Haill blosome breking out of the blud royall,
Quhois pretius vertew is imperiall.'

---

141 *denty*, favour   152 *macull*, spot; *doing spring*, arisen   155 *clarefeid*,
polished   157 *Quhill*, till   160 *hairbis*, plants   164 *mavys*, song-thrush

The merle scho sang, 'Haill Rois of most delyt,
Haill of all flouris quene and soverane;'   170
The lark scho song, 'Haill Rois both reid and quhyt,
Most plesand flour, of michty cullouris twane;'
The nychtingaill song, 'Haill naturis suffragene,
In bewty, nurtour and every nobilnes,
In riche array, renown and gentilnes.'   175

The commoun voce uprais of birdis small
Apone this wys, 'O blissit be the hour
That thow wes chosin to be our principall;
Welcome to be our princes of honour,
Our perle, our plesans, and our paramour,   180
Our peax, our play, our plane felicite,
Chryst the conserf frome all adversite.'

Than all the birdis song with sic a schout
That I annone awoilk quhair that I lay,
And with a braid I turnyt me about   185
To se this court, bot all wer went away.
Than up I lenyt, halflingis in affrey,
And thus I wret, as ye haif hard to forrow,
Off lusty May upone the nynt morrow.

173 *suffragene*, subordinate   181 *peax*, peace   185 *braid*, start   187 *halflingis*,
half   188 *to forrow*, before

8

3. ON HIS HEID-AKE

My heid did 3ak 3ester nicht,
This day to mak that I na micht.
So sair the magryme does me men3ie,
Persing my brow as ony gan3ie
That scant I luik may on the licht.   5

And now, schir, laitlie, efter mes,
To dyt thocht I begowthe to dres,
The sentence lay full evill till find,
Unsleipit in my heid behind,
Dullit in dulnes and distres.   10

Full oft at morrow I upryse,
Quhen that my curage sleiping lyis,
For mirth, for menstrallie and play,
For din nor danceing nor deray,
It will nocht walkin me no wise.   15

---

2 *mak*, write poetry   3 *magryme*, migraine; *men3ie*, hurt   4 *gan3ie*, dart
7 *dyt*, write   15 *walkin*, waken

9

This nycht, befoir the dawing cleir,
Me thocht Sanct Francis did to me appeir
With ane religious abbeit in his hand,
And said 'In this go cleith the, my servand;
Reffuss the warld, for thow mon be a freir.'   5

With him and with his abbeit bayth I skarrit
Lyk to ane man that with a gaist wes marrit;
Me thocht on bed he layid it me abone
Bot on the flure delyverly and sone
I lap thairfra, and nevir wald cum nar it.   10

Quoth he, 'Quhy skarris thow with this holy weid?
Cleith the thairin, for weir it thow most neid;
Thow that hes lang done Venus lawis teiche
Sall now be freir, and in this abbeit preiche;
Delay it nocht, it mon be done but dreid.'   15

Quod I 'Sanct Francis, loving be the till,
And thankit mot thow be of thy gude will
To me, that of thy clayis ar so kynd,
Bot thame to weir it nevir come in my mynd;
Sweit Confessour, thow tak it nocht in ill.   20

In haly legendis haif I hard allevin
Ma sanctis of bischoppis nor freiris, be sic sevin;
Off full few freiris that hes bene sanctis I reid;
Quhairfoir ga bring to me ane bischopis weid
Gife evir thow wald my sawle gaid unto hevin.'   25

6 *skarrit*, was scared   7 *marrit*, frightened   8 *abone*, above   9 *delyverly*,
promptly   21 *allevin*, alleged

'My brethir oft hes maid the supplicationis,
Be epistillis, sermonis, and relationis,
To tak the abyte, bot thow did postpone;
But ony process cum on thairfoir annone,
All sircumstance put by and excusationis'.   30

'Gif evir my fortoun wes to be a freir,
The dait thairof is past full mony a ȝeir;
For into every lusty toun and place
Off all Yngland, frome Berwick to Kalice,
I haif in to thy habeit maid gud cheir.   35

'In freiris weid full fairly haif I fleichit,
In it haif I in pulpet gon and preichit
In Derntoun kirk and eik in Canterberry;
In it I past at Dover our the ferry
Throw Piccardy, and thair the peple teichit.   40

Als lang as I did beir the freiris style,
In me, God wait, wes mony wrink and wyle;
In me wes falset with every wicht to flatter,
Quhilk mycht be flemit with na haly watter;
I wes ay reddy all men to begyle'.   45

This freir that did Sanct Francis thair appeir,
Ane fieind he wes in liknes of ane freir;
He vaneist away with stynk and fyrie smowk;
With him me thocht all the hous end he towk,
And I awoik as wy that wes in weir.   50

29 *but ony process*, without any argument   36 *fleichit*, fawned   42 *wrink*, trick
44 *flemit*, banished   50 *wy*, man; *weir*, doubt

11

Schir I complane off injuris,
A refing sonne off rakyng Muris
Hes magellit my making, throw his malis,
And present it in to ʒowr palis:
Bot, sen he plesis with me to pleid,   5
I sall him knawin mak hyne to Calis,
    Bot giff ʒowr Henes it remeid.

That fulle dismemberit hes my meter
And poysonid it with strang salpeter,
With rycht defamowss speiche off lordis   10
Quhilk with my collouris all discordis,
Quhois crewall sclander servis ded,
And in my name all leis recordis;
    ʒour Grace beseik I of remeid.

He has indorsit myn indyting   15
With versis off his awin hand wryting
Quhairin baithe sclander is and tressoun
Off ane wod fuill far owt off ressoun;
He wantis nocht bot a rowndit heid
For he has tynt baith wit and ressoun;   20
    ʒour Grace beseik I off remeid.

Puness him for his deid culpabile
Or gar deliver him a babile,
That Cuddy Rug, the Drumfres fuill,
May him resave agane this ʒuill,   25
All roundit in to ʒallow and reid;
That ladis may bait him lyk a buill,
    For that to me war sum remeid.

2 *refing*, thieving; *rakyng*, vagabond   3 *magellit*, mangled; *making*, poetry   6
hyne to Calis, from here to Calais   12 *servis ded*, deserves death   18 *wod*, mad
23 *babile*, bauble

6. ANE HIS AWIN ENNEMY

He that hes gold and grit riches,
And may be into mirryness,
And dois glaidness fra him expell,
And levis in to wrechitness,
 He wirkis sorrow to him sell.   5

He that may be but sturt or stryfe
And leif ane lusty plesand lyfe,
And syne with mariege dois him mell,
And bindis him with ane wicket wyfe,
 He wirkis sorrow to him sell.   10

He that hes for his awin genȝie
Ane plesand prop, but mank or menȝie,
And schuttis syne at ane uncow schell,
And is forfairn with the fleis of Spenȝie,
 He wirkis sorrow to him sell.   15

And he that with gud lyfe and trewth,
But varians or uder slewth,
Dois evir mair with ane maister dwell,
That nevir of him will haif no rewth,
 He wirkis sorrow to him sell.   20

Now all this tyme lat us be mirry,
And sett nocht by this warld a chirry;
Now quhill thair is gude wyne to sell,
He that dois on dry breid wirry,
 I gif him to the devill of hell.   25

---

6 *sturt*, discord 11 *genȝie*, disposition 12 *prop*, target; *but mank or menȝie*,
without flaw or stain 13 *uncow schell*, unknown target 14 *forfairn*, worn
out; *fleis of Spenȝie*, the Spanish fly 19 *rewth*, pity

THE FLYING OF DUNBAR AND KENNEDIE (extracts)

Quod Dunbar to Kennedy
Schir Johine the Ross, ane thing thair is compild
In generale be Kennedy and Quinting,
Quhilk hes thame self aboif the sternis styld;
Bot had thay maid of mannace ony mynting
In speciall, sic stryfe sould rys but stynting;   5
Howbeit with bost thair breistis wer als bendit
As Lucifer, that fra the hevin descendit,
Hell sould nocht hyd their harnis fra harmis hynting.

The erd sould trymbill, the firmament sould schaik,
And all the air in vannaum suddane stink,   10
And all the divillis of hell for redour quaik,
To heir quhat I sould wryt with pen and ynk;
For and I flyt sum sege for schame sould sink,
The se sould birn, the mone sould thoill ecclippis,
Rochis sould ryfe, the warld sould hald no grippis,   15
Sa loud of cair the commoun bell sould clynk.

Bot wondir laith wer I to be ane baird,
Flyting to use for gritly I eschame;
For it is nowthir wynning nor rewaird,
Bot tinsale baith of honour and of fame,   20
Incress of sorrow, sklander, and evill name;
3it mycht thay be sa bald, in thair bakbytting,
To gar me ryme and rais the feynd with flytting,
And throw all cuntreis and kinrikis thame proclame.

---

4 *mynting*, threat   8 *harnis*, brains; *hynting*, receiving   10 *vannaum*, venom
11 *redour*, fear   13 *sege*, man   15 *rochis sould ryfe*, rocks would split   17 *laith*,
reluctant   20 *tinsale*, loss, forfeiture   24 *kinrikis*, kingdoms

Quod Kennedy to Dunbar

Dirtin Dumbar, quhome on blawis thow thy boist, 25
Pretendand the to wryte sic skaldit skrowis?
Rawmowit rebald, thow fall doun att the roist,
My laureat lettres at the and I lowis;
Mandrag mymmerkin, maid maister bot in mows,
Thrys scheild trumpir with ane threid bair goun, 30
Say *Deo mercy*, or I cry the doun,
And leif thy ryming, rebald, and thy rowis.

Dreid, dirtfast dearch, that thow hes dissobeyit
My cousing Quintene and my commissar,
Fantastik fule, trest weill thow salbe fleyit, 35
Ignorant elf, aip, owll irregular,
Skaldit skaitbird, and commoun skamelar;
Wanfukkit funling, that natour maid ane yrle,
Baith Johine the Ros and thow sall squeill and skirle,
And evir I heir ocht of ȝour making mair. 40

Heir I put sylence to the in all pairtis,
Obey and ceis the play that thow pretendis;
Waik walidrag, and werlot of the cairtis,
Se sone thow mak my commissar amendis,
And lat him lay sax leichis on thy lendis, 45
Meikly in recompansing of thi scorne,
Or thow sall ban the tyme that thow wes borne,
For Kennedy to the this cedull sendis.

Juge in the nixt quha gat the war

26 *skaldit skrowis*, libellous scrolls   27 *roist*, encounter   28 *and I lowis*, if I
discharge   29 *mandrag mymmerkin*, mandrake mannikin; *mows*, jests   30
scheild, shelled, husked; *trumpir*, deceiver   32 *rowis*, rolls   33 *dearch*, dwarf
37 *skaitbird*, Arctic gull or dunghunter; *skamelar*, sponger   38 *wanfukkit funling*,
ill-begotten foundling; *yrle*, dwarf   40 *making*, poetry   43 *walidrag*, sloven;
werlot, varlet, knave   45 *leichis*, lashes; *lendis*, loins   48 *cedull*, schedule

Iersch brybour baird, vyle beggar with thy brattis,
Cuntbittin crawdoun Kennedy, coward of kynd,   50
Evill farit and dryit, as Denseman on the rattis,
Lyke as the gleddis had on thy gule snowt dynd;
Mismaid monstour, ilk mone owt of thy mynd,
Renunce, rebald, thy ryming, thow bot royis,
Thy trechour tung hes tane ane heland strynd;   55
Ane lawland ers wald mak a bettir noyis.

Revin raggit ruke, and full of rebaldrie,
Scarth fra scorpione, scaldit in scurrilitie,
I se the haltane in thy harlotrie,
And in to uthir science no thing slie,   60
Off every vertew voyd, as men may sie;
Quytclame clergie, and cleik to the ane club,
Ane baird blasphemar in brybrie ay to be;
For wit and wisdome ane wisp fra the may rub.

Thow speiris, dastard, gif I dar with the fecht?   65
3e dagone dowbart, thairof haif thow no dowt!
Quhair evir we meit, thairto my hand I hecht
To red thy rebald ryming with a rowt:
Throw all Bretane it salbe blawin owt
How that thow, poysonit pelor, gat thy paikis;   70
With ane doig leich I schepe to gar the schowt,
And nowther to the tak knyfe, swerd, nor aix.

Thow crop and rute of traitouris tressonable,
The fathir and moder of morthour and mischeif,
Dissaitfull tyrand with serpentis tung, unstable,   75
Cukcald cradoun, cowart, and commoun theif;
Thow purpest for to undo the Lord thy cheif,
In Paislay, with ane poysone that wes fell,
For quhilk, brybour, 3it sall thow thoill a breif;
Pelour, on the I sall it preif my sell.   80

---

49 *brybour*, beggar; *brattis*, rags   50 *cuntbittin*, poxy; *crawdoun*, coward   51
Denseman on the rattis, Dane executed on the wheel   52 *gleddis*, hawks; *gule
snowt*, yellow snout   54 *royis*, ravest   55 *strynd*, strain, race   57 *revin*, torn
58 *scarth*, hybrid monster   59 *haltane*, haughty; *harlotrie*, vileness   60 *slie*,
cunning   62 *quytclame*, give up   63 *brybrie*, beggary   65 *speiris*, ask   66
dagone dowbart, devil blockhead   68 *red*, correct; *rowt*, blow   70 *pelor*, thief;
paikis, punishment   77 *purpest*, purposed

Thocht I wald lie, thy frawart phisnomy
Dois manifest thy malice to all men;
Fy, tratour theif; fy, glengoir loun, fy fy!
Fy, feyndly front, far fowlar than ane fen.
My freyindis thow reprovit with thy pen;   85
Thow leis, tratour, quhilk I sall on the preif,
Suppois thy heid war armit tymis ten,
Thow sall recryat, or thy croun sall cleif.

Or thow durst move thy mynd malitius,
Thow saw the saill abone my heid up draw;   90
Bot Eolus full woid, and Neptunus,
Mirk and moneless, wes met with wind and waw,
And mony hundreth myle hyne cowd us blaw
By Holland, Seland, ʒetland, and Northway coist,
In desert quhair we were famist aw;   95
ʒit come I hame, fals baird, to lay thy boist.

Thow callis the rethory with thy goldin lippis:
Na, glowrand gaipand fule, thow art begyld,
Thow art bot gluntoch with thy giltin hippis,
That for thy lounry mony a leisch hes fyld;   100
Wan wisaged widdefow, out of thy wit gane wyld,
Laithly and lowsy, als lathand as ane leik,
Sen thow with wirschep wald sa fane be styld,
Haill, soverane senʒeour! Thy bawis hingis throw thy breik.

Forworthin fule, of all the warld reffuse,   105
Quhat ferly is thocht thow rejoys to flyte?
Sic eloquence as they in Erschry use,
In sic is sett thy thraward appetyte;
Thow hes full littill feill of fair indyte:
I tak on me ane pair of Lowthiane hippis   110
Sall fairar Inglis mak, and mair parfyte,
Than thow can blabbar with thy Carrik lippis.

---

81 *phisnomy*, face   83 *glengoir*, poxy   84 *fen*, mire, midden   88 *recryat*,
surrender   92 *waw*, wave   97 *rethory*, rhetorician   99 *gluntoch*, bare-kneed
100 *lounry*, knavery; *leisch*, leash; *fyld*, dirtied   101 *wan wisaged widdefow*,
leaden-faced gallows-bird   102 *lathand*, disgusting   104 *bawis*, balls   105
forworthin, deformed   106 *ferly*, wonder

17

Bettir thow ganis to leid ane doig to skomer,
Pynit pykpuris pelour, than with thy maister pingill.
Thow lay full prydles in the heit of summer,　　　　　115
And fane at evin for to bring hame a single,
Syne rubbit at ane uthir auld wyvis ingle;
Bot now, in winter, for purteth thow art traikit;
Thow hes na breik to latt thy bellokis gyngill;
Beg the ane club, for, baird, thow sall go naikit.　　　120

Lene larbar, loungeour, baith lowsy in lisk and lonȝe;
Fy, skolderit skyn, thow art bot skyre and skrumple;
For he that rostit Lawarance had thy grunȝe,
And he that hid Sanct Johnis ene with ane wimple,
And he that dang Sanct Augustine with ane rumple,　　125
Thy fowll front had, and he that Bartilmo flaid;
The gallowis gaipis eftir thy graceles gruntill,
As thow wald for ane haggeis, hungry gled.

Commirwald crawdoun, na man comptis the ane kerss,
Sueir swappit swanky, swynekeper ay for swaittis;　　130
Thy commissar Quintyne biddes the cum kis his erss,
He luvis nocht sic ane forlane loun of laittis;
He sayis, thow skaffis and beggis mair beir and aitis
Nor any cripill in Karrik land abowt;
Uther pure beggaris and thow ar at debaittis,　　　135
Decrepit karlingis on Kennedy cryis owt.

---

113 *ganis*, are fitted; *skomer*, defecate　　114 *pynit pykpuris pelour*, shrunken
pickpurse thief; *pingill*, strive　　115 *prydles*, without pride　　116 *single*, small
bundle of gleanings　　118 *purteth*, poverty; *traikit*, worn out　　121 *larbar*,
impotent man; *loungeour*, lay-about; *lisk*, groin; *lonȝe*, loin　　122 *skolderit*,
scorched; *skyre and skrumple*, wrinkles　　123 *grunȝe*, snout　　125 *rumple*, tail
127 *gruntill*, snout　　128 *gled*, kite　　129 *commirwald crawdoun*, henpecked
coward; *kerss*, cress　　130 *sueir swappit swanky*, lazy great fellow; *swaittis*, small
beer　　132 *forlane*, worthless　　133 *skaffis*, beg, sponge　　136 *karlingis*, old
women

Mater annuche I haif, I bid nocht fenȝie,
Thocht thow, fowll trumpour, thus upoun me leid;
Corruptit carioun, heir sall I cry thy senȝie;
Thinkis thow nocht how thow come in grit neid,   140
Grietand in Galloway, lyk to any gallow breid,
Ramand and rolpand, beggand koy and ox;
I saw the thair, in to thy wachemanis weid,
Quhilk wes nocht worth ane pair of auld gray sox.

Ersch Katherene, with thy polk breik and rilling,   145
Thow and thy quene, as gredy gleddis, ȝe gang
With polkis to mylne, and beggis baith meill and schilling;
Thair is bot lys and lang nailis ȝow amang:
Fowll heggirbald, for hennis ȝit will ȝe hang;
Thow hes ane perrellus face to play with lambis;   150
Ane thowsand kiddis, wer thay in faldis full strang,
Thy lymmerfull luke wald fle thame and their damis.

In till ane glen thow hes, owt of repair,
Ane laithly luge that wes the lippir menis;
With the ane sowtaris wyfe, off blis als bair,   155
And lyk twa stalkaris steilis in cokis and hennis,
Thow plukkis the pultre, and scho pullis off the penis;
All Karrik cryis, God gif this dowsy be drownd;
And quhen thow heiris ane guse cry in the glenis,
Thow thinkis it swetar than sacryne bell of sound.   160

Thow Lazarus, thow laithly lene tramort,
To all the warld thow may example be,
To luk upoun thy gryslie peteous port,
For hiddowis, haw and holkit is thyne ee;
Thy cheik bane bair, and blaiknit is thy ble;   165
Thy choip, thy choll, garris men for to leif chest;
Thy gane it garris us think that we mon de:
I conjure the, thow hungert heland gaist.

137 *fenȝie*, feign   139 *senȝie*, warcry   141 *gallow breid*, born to be hanged
142 *ramand and rolpand*, shouting and roaring; *koy*, cows   145 *polk breik*, tartan
bag; *rilling*, shoes of undressed hide   146 *quene*, hussy   147 *schilling*, husks
of grain   149 *heggirbald*, obscure insult   152 *lymmerfull*, villainous; *fle*, scare
154 *luge*, dwelling   155 *sowtar*, cobbler   156 *stalkaris*, poachers   158 *dowsy*, fool
161 *tramort*, rotting corpse   164 *haw and holkit*, livid and hollowed   165
blaiknit, pallid   166 *choip*, jaw; *choll*, jowl; *chest*, chaste   167 *gane*, ugly face

19

The larbar lukis of thy lang lene craig,
Thy pure pynit thrott, peilit and owt of ply,   170
Thy skolderit skin, hewd lyk ane saffrone bag,
Garris men dispyt thar flesche, thow Spreit of Gy:
Fy, feyndly front; fy, tykis face, fy fy!
Ay loungand, lyk any loikman on ane ledder;
With hingit luik ay wallowand upone wry,   175
Lyke to ane stark theif glowrand in ane tedder.

Nyse nagus, nipcaik, with thy schulderis narrow,
Thow lukis lowsy, loun of lownis aw;
Hard hurcheoun, hirpland, hippit as any harrow,
Thy rigbane rattilis, and thy ribbis on raw,   180
Thy hanchis hirklis with hukebanis harth and haw,
Thy laithly lymis are lene as ony treis;
Obey, theif baird, or I sall brek thy gaw,
Fowll carrybald, cry mercy on thy kneis.

Thow pure pynhippit ugly averill,   185
With hurkland banis, holkand throw thy hyd,
Reistit and crynit as hangitman on hill,
And oft beswakkit with ane ourhie tyd,
Quhilk brewis mekle barret to thy bryd;
Hir cair is all to clenge thy cabroch howis,   190
Quhair thow lyis sawsy in saphron, bak and syd,
Powderit with prymros, sawrand all with clowis.

---

169 *larbar*, weak   171 *skolderit*, scorched   173 *tykis*, cur's   174 *loungand*,
slouching; *loikman*, hangman   175 *upone wry*, awry   176 *tedder*, noose
177 *nagus*, stingy fellow; *nipcaik*, miser   179 *hurcheoun*, hedgehog; *hirpland*,
limping   180 *rigbane*, backbone   181 *hirklis* huddles; *hukebanis*, hucklebones
183 *gaw*, gall-bladder   184 *carrybald*, cannibal   185 *pynhippit*, lean-hipped;
averill, carthorse   186 *holkand*, poking   187 *reistit*, dried; *crynit*, shrivelled
188 *beswakkit*, drenched; *tyd*, tide   189 *barret*, trouble   190 *cabroch*, scraggy;
howis, hocks   191 *sawsy*, sauced   192 *sawrand*, smelling; *clowis*, cloves

20

Forworthin wirling, I warne the it is wittin,
How, skyttand skarth, thow hes the hurle behind;
Wan wraiglane wasp, ma wormis hes thow beschittin   195
Nor ther is gerss on grund or leif on lind;
Thocht thow did first sic foly to me fynd,
Thow sall agane with ma witness than I;
Thy gulsoch gane dois on thy back it bind,
Thy hostand hippis lattis nevir thy hos go dry.   200

Thow held the burgh lang wit ane borrowit goun,
And ane caprowsy barkit all with sweit,
And quhen the laidis saw the sa lyk a loun,
Thay bickerit the with mony bae and bleit:
Now upaland thow leivis on rubbit quheit,   205
Oft for ane caus thy burdclaith neidis no spredding,
For thow hes nowthir for to drink nor eit,
Bot lyk ane berdles baird that had no bedding.

Strait Gibbonis air, that nevir ourstred ane hors,
Bla berfute berne, in bair tyme wes thow borne;   210
Thow bringis the Carrik clay to Edinburgh Corss
Upoun thy botingis, hobland, hard as horne;
Stra wispis hingis owt, quhair that the wattis ar worne:
Cum thow agane to skar us with thy strais,
We sall gar scale our sculis all the to scorne,   215
And stane the up the calsay quhair thow gais.

Off Edinburgh the boyis as beis owt thrawis,
And cryis owt 'Hay, heir cumis our awin queir Clerk!'
Than fleis thow lyk ane howlat chest with crawis
Quhill all the bichis at thy botingis does bark: 220
Than carlingis cryis, 'Keip curches in the merk,
Our gallowis gaipis; lo! quhair ane greceles gais.'
Ane uthir sayis, 'I se him want ane sark,
I reid ʒow, cummer, tak in ʒour lynning clais.'

193 *wirling*, wretch   194 *skyttand*, shitting; *hurle behind*, diarrhoea   195
wraiglane, wriggling   197 *foly*, dirt   200 *hostand*, coughing   202 *caprowsy*,
short hooded cloak   203 *loun*, wretch   204 *bickerit*, assailed; *bae and bleit*, baa
and bleat   205 *upaland*, in the country   206 *burdclaith*, tablecloth   209 *strait*,
stingy; *air*, heir   210 *berne*, fellow   212 *botingis*, boots   213 *wattis*, welts
215 *scale*, disperse from   216 *calsay*, street   217 *thrawis*, throng   219 *howlat*, owl;
chest with crawis, chased by crows   221 *curches*, kerchiefs; *in the merk*, out of sight

Than rynis thow doun the gait with gild of boyis,   225
And all the toun tykis hingand in thy heilis;
Of laidis and lownis thair rysis sic ane noyis,
Quhill runsyis rynis away with cairt and quheilis,
And cager aviris castis bayth coilis and creilis,
For rerd of the and rattling of thy butis;   230
Fische wyvis cryis, Fy! and castis doun skillis and skeilis;
Sum claschis the, sum cloddis the on the cutis.

Loun lyk Mahoun, be boun me till obey,
Theif, or in greif mischeif sall the betyd;
Cry grace, tykis face, or I the chece and fley;   235
Oule, rare and ʒowle, I sall defowll thy pryd;
Peilit gled, baith fed and bred of bichis syd,
And lyk ane tyk, purspyk, quhat man settis by the,
Forflittin, countbittin, beschittin, barkit hyd,
Clym ledder, fyle tedder, foule edder, I defy the.   240

Mauch muttoun, byt buttoun, peilit gluttoun, air to Hilhous;
Rank beggar, ostir dregar, foule fleggar in the flet;
Chittirlilling, ruch rilling, lik schilling in the milhous;
Baird rehator, theif of nator, fals tratour, feyindis gett;
Filling of tauch, rak sauch, cry crauch, thow art oursett; 245
Muttoun dryver, girnall ryver, ʒadswyvar, fowll fell the:
Herretyk, lunatyk, purspyk, carlingis pet,
Rottin crok, dirtin dok, cry cok, or I sall quell the.

---

225 *gild*, clamour   228 *runsyis*, horses   229 *aviris*, carthorses; *coilis and creilis*,
coals and baskets   230 *rerd*, din   231 *skillis and skeilis*, wicker platters and
tubs   232 *cutis*, ankles   237 *peilit gled*, plucked kite   238 *purspyk*,
pickpocket   239 *forflittin*, out-flyted; *countbittin*, poxy; *barkit*, tanned   240
clym, climb; *fyle tedder*, defile the noose   241 *mauch*, maggot   242 *ostir dregar*,
oyster dredger; *fleggar*, flatterer; *flet*, inner part of house   243 *chittirlilling*,
obscure term of abuse; *ruch rilling*, hairy shoes of skin; *schilling*, husks of grain
244 *rehator*, villain   245 *tauch*, tallow; *rak sauch*, stretch the withy; *crauch*,
beaten; *oursett*, defeated   246 *ʒadswyvar*, mare-buggerer   247 *carlingis*, old
women   248 *dok*, arse; *cry cok*, admit defeat

8. MEDITATIOUN IN WYNTIR

In to thir dirk and drublie dayis,
Quhone sabill all the hewin arrayis
With mystie vapouris, cluddis, and skyis
Nature all curage me denyis
Off sangis, ballattis, and of playis.   5

Quhone that the nycht dois lenthin houris
With wind, with haill, and havy schouris,
My dule spreit dois lurk for schoir,
My hairt for languor dois forloir
For laik of Symmer with his flouris.   10

I walk, I turne, sleip may I nocht,
I vexit am with havie thocht;
This warld all ouir I cast about,
And ay the mair I am in dout,
The mair that I remeid have socht.   15

I am assayit on euerie syde:
Despair sayis ay, 'In tyme provyde
And get sum thing quhairon to leif,
Or with grit trouble and mischeif
Thow sall in to this court abyd.'   20

Than Patience sayis, 'Be not agast:
Hald Hoip and Treuthe within the fast,
And lat Fortoun wirk furthe hir rage,
Quhome that no rasoun may assuage,
Quhill that hir glas be run and past.'   25

And Prudence in my eir sayis ay
'Quhy wald thow hald that will away?
Or craif that thow may have no space,
Thow tending to ane uther place,
A journay going everie day?'   30

---

1 *drublie*, clouded   8 *dule*, grief; *schoir*, menace   9 *forloir*, feel forlorn

And than sayis Age, 'My freind, cum neir,
And be not strange, I the requeir:
Cum, brodir, by the hand me tak,
Remember thow hes compt to mak
Off all thi tyme thow spendit heir.'   35

Syne Deid castis upe his ʒettis wyd,
Saying, 'Thir oppin sall the abyd;
Albeid that thow wer neuer sa stout,
Undir this lyntall sall thow lowt,
Thair is nane uther way besyde.'   40

For feir of this all day I drowp,
No gold in kist, nor wyne in cowp,
No ladeis bewtie, not luiffis blys,
May lat me to remember this,
How glaid that ever I dyne or sowp.   45

ʒit quhone the nycht begynnis to schort
It does my spreit sum pairt confort,
Off thocht oppressit with the schowris;
Cum lustie Symmer with thi flowris,
That I may leif in sum disport.   50

32 *strange*, aloof   39 *lowt*, bow   44 *lat*, prevent

Off every asking followis nocht
Rewaird, bot gif sum caus war wrocht;
And quhair caus is, men weill ma sie,
And quhair nane is, it wilbe thocht,
    In asking sowld discretioun be.   5

Ane fule, thocht he haif caus or nane,
Cryis ay, 'Gif me', in to a drene;
And he that dronis ay as ane bee
Sowld haif ane heirar dull as stane;
    In asking sowld discretioun be.   10

Sum askis mair than he deservis,
Sum askis far les than he servis,
Sum schames to ask, as braidis of me,
And all withowt reward he stervis;
    In asking sowld discretioun be.   15

To ask but service hurtis gud fame;
To ask for service is not to blame;
To serve and leif in beggartie
To man and maistir is baith schame:
    In asking sowld discretion be.   20

He that does all his best servyis
May spill it all with crakkis and cryis,
Be fowll inoportunitie;
Few wordis may serve the wyis;
    In asking sowld discretioun be.   25

Nocht neidfull is men sowld be dum;
Na thing is gottin but wordis sum;
Nocht sped but diligence we se,
For nathing it allane will cum;
    In asking sowld discretioun be.   30

7 *drene*, drone   9 *heirar*, hearer   13 *as braidis of me*, as my nature is   14
stervis, perishes

Asking wald haif convenient place,
Convenient tyme, lasar and space,
But haist or preis of grit menȝie,
But hairt abasit, but toung rekles;
    In asking sowld discretioun be.   35

Sum micht haif 'ȝe' with littill cure
That hes oft 'nay' with grit labour;
All for that tyme not byd can he,
He tynis baith eirand and honour:
    In asking sowld discretioun be.   40

Suppois the servand be lang unquit,
The lord sumtyme rewaird will it;
Gife he does not, quhat remedy?
To fecht with fortoun is no wit;
    In asking sowld discretioun be.   45

32 *lasar*, leisure   33 *menȝie*, company of people   39 *eirand*, business

10. OF DISCRETIOUN IN GEVING

To speik of gift or almous deidis,
Sum gevis for mereit and for meidis;
Sum, warldly honour to uphie,
Gevis to thame that no thing neidis:
    In geving sowld discretioun be.   5

Sum gevis for pryd and glory vane,
Sum gevis with grugeing and with pane;
Sum gevis in practik for supple;
Sum gevis for twyis als gud agane:
    In geving sowld discretioun be.   10

Sum gevis for thank, sum for threit;
Sum gevis money, and sum gevis meit;
Sum gevis wordis fair and sle;
Giftis fra sum ma na man treit;
    In giving sowld discretioun be.   15

Sum is for gift sa lang requyrd
Quhill that the crevar be so tyrd
That, or the gift deliverit be,
The thank is frustrat and expyrd:
    In geving sowld discretioun be.   20

Sum gevis to littill full wretchitly,
That his giftis ar not set by
And for a huidpyk haldin is he,
That all the warld cryis on him, Fy;
    In geving sowld discretioun be.   25

Sum in his geving is so large,
That all ourlaidin is his berge;
Than vyce and prodigalite
Thairof his honour dois dischairge;
    In geving sowld discretioun be.   30

---

2 *meidis*, reward   3 *uphie*, exalt   8 *practik*, policy; *supple*, self-interest
13 *sle*, cunning   14 *treit*, have dealings with   17 *crevar*, one who craves
23 *huidpyk*, miser   27 *berge*, barge

Sum to the riche gevis geir,
That micht his giftis weill forbeir;
And thocht the peur for falt sowld de,
His cry nocht enteris in his eir:
    In geving sowld discretioun be.   35

Sum givis to strangeris with face new,
That ʒisterday fra Flanderis flew,
And to awld serwandis list not se,
War thay nevir of sa grit vertew;
    In geving sowld discretioun be.   40

Sum gevis to thame can ask and plenʒie,
Sum gevis to thame can flattir and fenʒie,
Sum gevis to men of honestie,
And haldis all janglaris at disdenʒie;
    In geving sowld discretioun be.   45

Sum gettis giftis and riche arrayis
To sweir all that his maister sayis,
Thocht all the contrair weill knawis he;
Ar mony sic now in thir dayis;
    In geving sowld discretioun be.   50

Sum gevis gud men for thair gud kewis;
Sum gevis to trumpouris and to schrewis;
Sum gevis to knaiffis awtoritie;
Bot in thair office gude fundin few is:
    In geving sowld discretioun be.   55

Sum givis parrochynnis full wyd,
Kirkis of Sanct Barnard and Sanct Bryd,
To teiche, to rewill, and to ouirsie,
That he na wit hes thame to gyd;
    In geving sowld discretioun be.   60

33 *peur*, poor; *for falt*, for want   52 *trumpouris*, cheats   56 *parrochynnis*,
parishes

11.   OF DISCRETIOUN IN TAKING

Eftir geving I speik of taking,
Bot littill of ony gud forsaiking.
Sum takkis our littill awtoritie,
And sum our mekle, and that is glaiking;
    In taking sowld discretioun be.   5

The clerkis takis beneficis with brawlis,
Sum of Sanct Petir, and sum of Sanct Pawlis;
Tak he the rentis, no cair hes he,
Suppois the divill tak all thair sawlis;
    In taking sowld discretioun be.   10

Barronis takis fra the tennentis peure
All fruct that growis on the feure,
In mailis and gersomes rasit ouirhie,
And garris thame beg fra dur to dure:
    In taking sowld discretioun be.   15

[Thir merchandis takis unlesum win
Quhilk makis thair pakkis oftymes full thin
Be thair successioun ʒe may see
That ill won geir riches not the kin
    In taking sowld discretioun be]   20

Sum takis uthir menis takkis,
And on the peure oppressioun makkis,
And nevir remembris that he mon die,
Quhill that the gallowis gar him rax;
    In taking sowld discretioun be.   25

Sum takis be sie and be land,
And nevir fra taking can hald thair hand,
Quhill he be tit up to ane tre;
And syne they gar him undirstand
    In taking sowld discretioun be.   30

---

4 *mekle*, much; *glaiking*, folly   12 *feure*, furrow   13 *mailis and gersomes*, rents
and additional rents   16 *unlesum win*, unlawful profit   21 *takkis*, leasehold
land   24 *gar him rax*, make him stretch

Sum wald tak all his nychbouris geir,
Had he of man als littill feir
As he hes dreid that God him see;
To tak than sowld he nevir forbeir:
    In taking sowld discretioun be.   35

[Stude I na mair aw of man nor god
Than suld I tak bayth ewin and od
Ane end to all thing that I see
Sic iustice is not worthe ane clod
    In taking sowld discretioun be.]   40

Sum wald tak all this warldis breid,
And ȝit not satisfeit of thair neid,
Throw hairt unsatiable and gredie;
Sum wald tak littill, and can not speid:
    In taking sowld discretioun be.   45

Grit men for taking and oppressioun
Ar sett full famous at the Sessioun,
And peur takaris ar hangit hie,
Schamit for evir and thair successioun;
    In taking sowld discretioun be.   50

48 *takaris*, leaseholders

Schir, 3e have mony servitouris
And officiaris of dyuers curis:
Kirkmen, courtmen, and craftismen fyne,
Doctouris in jure and medicyne,
Divinouris, rethoris, and philosophouris,   5
Astrologis, artistis, and oratouris;
Men of armes, and vail3eand knychtis,
And mony vther gudlie wichtis;
Musicianis, menstralis, and mirrie singaris,
Chevalouris, cawandaris, and [   ] flingaris;   10
Cun3ouris, carvouris, and carpentaris,
Beildaris of barkis and ballingaris,
Masounis lyand upon the land,
And schipwrichtis hewand vpone the strand;
Glasing wrichtis, goldsmythis, and lapidaris,   15
Pryntouris, payntouris, and potingaris,
And all of thair craft cunning,
And all at anis lawboring,
Quhilk pleisand ar and honorable,
And to 3our hienes profitable,   20
And richt convenient for to be
With 3our hie regale majestie;
Deserving of 3our grace most ding
Bayth thank, rewarde, and cherissing.

And thocht that I, amang the laif,   25
Vnworthy be ane place to haue,
Or in thair nummer to be tald,
Als lang in mynd my wark sall hald,
Als haill in everie circumstance,
In forme, in mater, and substance,   30
But wering or consumptioun,
Roust, canker, or corruptioun,
As ony of thair werkis all,
Suppois that my rewarde be small.

10 *cawandaris*, entertainers; *flingaris*, dancers   11 *cun3ouris*, coiners   12
ballingaris, small ships   15 *lapidaris*, jewellers   16 *potingaris*, apothecaries
23 *ding*, worthy

Bot ʒe sa gracious ar and meik,   35
That on ʒour hienes followis eik
Ane vthir sort, more miserabill,
Thocht thai be nocht sa profitable:
Fenʒeouris, fleichouris, and flatteraris,
Cryaris, craikaris, and clatteraris,   40
Soukaris, groukaris, gledaris, gunnaris,
Mousouris of France, gud clarat-cunnaris,
Innopportoun askaris of Yrland kynd,
And meit revaris, lyk out of mynd;
Scaffaris and scamleris in the nuke,   45
And hall huntaris of draik and duik;
Thrimlaris and thristaris, as thay war woid,
Kokenis, and kennis na man of gude;
Schulderaris, and schowaris, that hes no schame,
And to no cunning that can clame,   50
And can non vthir craft nor curis
Bot to mak thrang, Schir, in ʒour duris,
And rusche in quhair thay counsale heir,
And will at na man nurtir leyr.
In quintiscence, eik, ingynouris joly,   55
That far can multiplie in folie,
Fantastik fulis, bayth fals and gredy,
Off toung untrew, and hand evill deidie:
Few dar, of all this last additioun,
Cum in tolbuyth without remissoun.   60

---

39 *fenʒeouris*, dissimulators; *fleichouris*, cajolers   40 *cryeris*, those who shout for
themselves; *craikaris*, noisy fellows; *clatteraris*, chatterers   41 *soukaris*, parasites;
groukaris, those who spy suspiciously on others   42 *cunnaris*, tasters   45
scaffaris and scamleris, beggars and spongers   46 *hall huntaris*, scroungers of
hospitality   47 *thrimlaris and thristaris*, hustlers and thrusters   48 *kokenis*,
rogues   49 *schulderaris and schowaris*, pushers and shovers   55 *quintiscence*,
alchemy; *eik*, also; *ingynouris*, alchemists

And thocht this nobill cunning sort,
Quhom of befoir I did report,
Rewardit be, it war bot ressoun,
Thairat suld no man mak enchessoun;
Bot quhen the vther fulis nyce,   65
That feistit at Cokelbeis gryce,
Ar all rewardit, and nocht I,
Than on this fals world I cry Fy.
My hart neir bristis than for teyne,
Quhilk may nocht suffer nor sustene   70
So grit abusioun for to se
Daylie in court befoir myn E.
And ȝit more panence wald I haue,
Had I rewarde among the laif;
It wald me sumthing satisfie,   75
And less of my malancolie,
And gar me mony falt ourse,
That now is brayd befoir myn E:
My mind so fer is set to flyt
That of nocht ellis I can endyt,   80
For owther man my hart to breik,
Or with my pen I man me wreik;
And sen the tane most nedis be,
In to malancolie to de,
And lat the vennim ische all out,   85
Be war anone, for it will spout
Gif that the tryackill cum nocht tyt
To swage the swalme of my dispyt.

64 *enchessoun*, objection   69 *teyne*, grief   87 *tryackill*, remedy; *tyt*, quickly
88 *swalme*, swelling

That he war Johne Thomsounis Man

Schir for 3our Grace bayth nicht and day
Richt hartlie on my kneis I pray
With all devotioun that I can,
    God gif 3e war Johne Thomsounis man!

For war it so, than weill war me, 5
But benefice I wald nocht be;
My hard fortoun wer endit than,
    God gif 3e war Johne Thomsounis man!

Than wald sum reuth within 3ow rest,
For saik of hir, fairest and best 10
In Bartane sen hir tyme began;
    God gif 3e war Johne Thomsounis man!

For it micht hurt in no degre,
That one so fair and gude as sche,
Throw hir vertew sic wirschip wan, 15
    Als 3ow to mak Johne Thomsounis man.

I wald gif all that ever I haue
To that conditioun, sa God me saif,
That 3e had vowit to the Swan
    Ane 3eir to be Johne Thomsounis man. 20

The mersy of that sweit meik rois
Suld soft 3ow, thirsill, I suppois,
Quhois pykis throw me so reuthles ran;
    God gif 3e war Johne Thomsounis man!

My aduocat, bayth fair and sweit, 25
The hale rejosing of my spreit,
Wald speid in to my erand than,
    And 3e war anis Johne Thomsounis man.

Ever quhen I think 3ow harde or dour
Or mercyles in my succour, 30
Than pray I god and sweit Sanct An,
    Gif that 3e war Johne Thomsounis man!

6 *but*, without   9 *reuth*, compassion   11 *Bartane*, Britain   21 *rois*, rose 22
thirsill, thistle   23 *pykis*, spines

14. TO THE LORDIS OF THE KINGIS CHALKER

My Lordis of Chalker, pleis ȝow to heir
My coumpt, I sall it mak ȝow cleir,
But ony circumstance or sonȝie;
For left is nether corce nor cunȝie
Off all that I tuik in the ȝeir.   5

For rekkyning of my rentis and roumes,
ȝe neid nocht for to tyre ȝour thowmes;
Na for to gar ȝour countaris clink,
Nor paper for to spend, nor ink,
In the ressaveing of my soumes.   10

I tuik fra my Lord Thesaurair
Ane soume of money for to wair:
I cannot tell ȝow how it is spendit,
Bot weill I waitt that it is endit;
And that me think ane coumpt our sair!   15

I trowit the tyme quhen that I tuik it,
That lang in burgh I sould have bruikit,
Now the remanes are eith to turs;
I have·na preiff heir bot my purs,
Quhilk wald nocht lie and it war luikit.   20

1 *Chalker*, exchequer   2 *coumpt*, account   3 *sonȝie*, excuse   4 *corce*, coin with
cross on one side; *cunȝie*, coin   6 *roumes*, property   12 *wair*, spend
17 *broukit*, enjoyed   18 *eith to turs*, easy to carry   20 *luikit*, inspected

15. TO THE KING

Schir 3e remembir as befoir,
How that my 3outhe is done forloir
In 3our seruice with pane and greiff;
Gud conscience cryis reward thairfoir;
Exces of thocht dois me mischeif.   5

3our clarkis ar servit all aboute,
And I do lyke ane rid halk schout
To cum to lure that hes na leif,
Quhair my plumis begynnis to mowt;
Exces of thocht dois me mischeiff.   10

For3et is ay the falcounis kynd,
Bot ever the myttell is hard in mynd;
Quhone the gled dois the peirtrikis preiff,
The gentill goishalk gois undynd;
Exces of thocht dois me mischeiff.   15

The pyat withe the pairtie cote
Feyn3eis to sing the nychtingale note,
Bot scho can not the corchet cleiff,
For hasknes of hir carleche throte;
Exces of thocht dois me mischeiff.   20

Ay fairast feddiris hes farrest foulis
Suppois thay haue na sang bot 3owlis;
In sylver caiges thai sit but greif;
Kynd native nestis dois clek bot owlis:
Exces of thocht dois me mischeiff.   25

O gentill egill, how may this be
Quhilk of all foulis dois heast fle,
3our leggis quhy do 3e nocht releif,
And chirreis thame eftir thair degre?
Exces of thocht dois me mischeiff.   30

---

2 *forloir*, destroyed   5 *thocht*, worry   12 *myttell*, bird of prey   13 *gled*, kite;
peirtrikis, partridges; *preiff*, taste   14 *goishalk*, goshawk   16 *pyat*, magpie
19 *carleche*, churlish   21 *farrest*, most distant   24 *clek*, hatch   28 *leggis*, lieges

Quhone servit is all vther man,
Gentill and sempill of everie clan,
Raf Coil3earis kynd and Johnne the Reif,
No thing I gett nor conqueis can;
    Exces of thocht dois me mischeif.   35

Thocht I in courte be maid refuse
And have few vertewis for to ruse,
3it am I cum of Adame and Eve,
And fane wald leif as vtheris dois;
    Exces of thocht dois me mischeif.   40

Or I suld leif in sic mischance,
Giff it to God war na grevance,
To be ane pykthank I wald preif
For thai in warld wantis na plesance;
    Exces of thocht dois me mischeif.   45

In sum pairt of my selffe I plein3e
Quhone vtheris dois flattir and feyn3e;
Allace, I can bot ballatis breif,
Sic barnheid leidis my brydill reyn3e;
    Exces of thocht dois me mischeiff.   50

I grant my seruice is bot lycht,
Thairfoir of mercye and not of rycht
I ask 3ou, Sir, no man to greiff,
Sum medecyne gif that 3e mycht;
    Exces of thocht dois me mischeiff.   55

Nane can remeid my maledie
Sa weill as 3e, Sir, veralie;
With ane benefice 3e may preiff,
And gif I mend not haistalie,
    Exces of thocht lat me mischeif.   60

34 *conqueis*, acquire   43 *pykthank*, one who curries favour   48 *breif*, write
49 *barnheid*, childishness

I wes in ȝouthe on nureice kne
Cald dandillie, bischop, dandillie,
And quhone that age now dois me greif,
A sempill vicar I can not be;
    Exces of thocht dois me mischeif.   65

Jok that wes wont to keip the stirkis
Can now draw him ane cleik of kirkis,
With ane fals cairt in to his sleif,
Worthe all my ballattis under the byrkis;
    Exces of thocht dois me mischeif.   70

Two curis or thre hes uplandis Michell,
With dispensationis in ane knitchell
Thocht he fra nolt had new tane leif;
He playis with *totum* and I with *nychell*:
    Exces of thocht dois me mischeiff.   75

How sould I leif and I not landit,
Nor ȝit withe benefice am blandit?
I say not, Sir, ȝow to repreiff,
Bot doutles I go rycht neir hand it:
    Exces of thocht dois me mischeiff.   80

As saule in to purgatorie,
Leifand in pane with hoip of glorie,
So is my selffe ȝe may belieff
In hoip, Sir, of ȝour adiutorie;
    Exces of thocht dois me mischeiff.   85

66 *stirkis*, young bullocks   67 *cleik*, hand of cards   69 *under the byrkis*, under the birch trees   72 *knitchell*, bundle   77 *blandit*, soothed

16. IN THIS WARLD MAY NONE ASSURE

Quhomto sall I compleine my wo
And kythe my cairis ane or mo?
I knaw not amang riche or pure
Quha is my freind, quha is my fo
   For in this warld may non assure.   5

Lord how sall I my dayis dispone
For lang service rewarde is none,
And schort my lyfe may heir indure
And losit is my tyme bigane;
   In to this warld may none assure.   10

Oft falsatt rydis with a rowtt
Quhone treuthe gois on his fute about,
And laik of spending dois him spure;
Thus quhat to do I am in dout,
   In to this warld may none assure.   15

Nane heir bot rich men hes renown
And pure men ar plukit doun
And nane bot just men tholis injure;
Swa wit is blyndit and ressoun
   For in this warld may none assure.   20

Vertew the court hes done dispys,
Ane rebald to renoun dois rys
And carlis of nobillis hes the cure,
And bumbardis brukis benefys;
   So in this warld may none assure.   25

All gentrice and nobilite
Ar passit out of hie degre,
On fredome is laid foirfalture;
In princis is thair no petie,
   So in this warld may none assure.   30

---

2 *kythe*, declare   11 *rowtt*, retinue   13 *spure*, prick   22 *rebald*, rascal   23 *cure*, pastoral charge   24 *bumbardis*, lazy fellow; *brukis*, enjoy

Is non so armit in to plait
That can fra trouble him debait;
May no man lang in welthe indure
For wo that lyis euer at the wait
    So in this warld may none assure.   35

Flattrie weiris ane furrit goun
And falsate with the lordis dois roun
And trewthe standis barrit at the dure,
Exylit is honour of the toun
    So in the warld may none assure.   40

Fra everie mouthe fair wordis procedis,
In everie harte deceptioun bredis,
Fra everie E gois lukis demure,
Bot fra the handis gois few gud deidis;
    Sa in this warld may none assure.   45

Towngis now are maid of quhite quhale bone
And hartis ar maid of hard flynt stone
And eyn ar maid of blew asure
And handis of adamant laithe to dispone;
    So in this warld may none assure.   50

3it hart and handis and body all
Mon anser dethe quhone he dois call
To compt befoir the juge future;
Sen al ar deid or de sall,
    Quha sould in to this warld assure?   55

No thing bot deithe this schortlie cravis
Quhair fortoun ever, as fo, dissavis
Withe freyndlie smylingis lyk ane hure
Quhais fals behechtis as wind hyne wavis,
    So in this warld may none assure.   60

31 *in to plait*, in steel plate   32 *debait*, defend   37 *roun*, whisper   54 *de sall*,
shall die   59 *behechtis*, promises; *hyne*, hence

O, quha sall weild the wrang possessioun
Or gadderit gold with oppressioun,
Quhone the angell blawis his bugill sture
Quhilk onrestorit helpis no confessioun?
   In to this warld may none assure.   65

Quhat help is thair in lordschips sevin
Quhone na hous is bot hell and hevin,
Palice of lycht, or pit obscure,
Quhair ȝowlis ar with horrible stevin?
   In to this warld may none assure.   70

Ubi ardentes anime
Semper dicentes sunt Ve! Ve!
Sall cry Allace, that women thame bure,
O quante sunt iste tenebre!
   In to this warld may none assure.   75

Than who sall wirk for warldis wrak
Quhone flude and fyre sall our it frak
And frelie frustir feild and fure
With tempest keyne and thundir crak?
   In to this warld may none assure.   80

Lord! sen in tyme sa sone to cum
De terra surrecturus sum,
Rewarde me with na erthlie cure
Bot me ressave *in regnum tuum,*
   Sen in this warld may non assure.   85

Schir, lat it nevir in toune be tald
That I suld be ane 3owllis 3ald!

Suppois I war ane ald 3ald aver
Schott furth our clewch to squische the clever
And hed the strenthis off all Strenever,   5
I wald at 3oull be housit and stald;
   Schir lat it never in toune be tald
   That I suld be ane 3owllis 3ald!

I am ane auld hors, as 3e knaw,
That ever in duill does drug and draw;   10
Great court hors puttis me fra the staw
To fang the fog be firthe and fald;
   Schir lat it never in toune be tald
   That I suld be ane 3owllis 3ald!

I heff run lang furth in the feild   15
On pastouris that ar plane and peld;
I mycht be now tein in for eild,
My bekis ar spruning he and bald;
   Schir lat it never in toun be tald
   That I suld be ane 3owllis 3ald!   20

My maine is turned in to quhyt
And thair off 3e heff all the wyt;
Quhen uthair hors hed brane to byt
I gat bot gris, grype giff I wald.
   Schir lat it never in towne be tald   25
   That I suld be ane 3owllis 3ald!

2 *3owllis 3ald*, old horse at Christmas   3 *3ald aver*, worn out cart-horse   4
clewch, ravine; *squische*, crush; *clever*, clover   5 *strenthis*, fastnesses; *Strenever*,
Strathnaver, Sutherland   10 *duill*, sorrow; *drug*, drudge   11 *staw*, stall   12
fang, take; *fog*, winter grass   15 *peld*, bare   16 *eild*, age   17 *bekis*, teeth;
spruning, sticking out   22 *wyt*, blame   24 *gris*, grass; *grype*, grip

I was never dautit in to stabell,
My lyff hes bein so miserabell,
My hyd to offer I am abell,
For evill schoud strae that I reiv wald.   30
    Schir lat it never in towne be tald
    That I suld be ane ʒowllis ʒald!

And ʒett, suppois my thrift be thyne,
Gif that I die ʒour aucht within,
Lat nevir the soutteris have my skin,   35
With uglie gumes to be gnawin.
    Schir lat it nevir in toun be tald
    That I suld be ane ʒowllis ʒald!

The court hes done my curage cuill
And maid me ane forriddin muill;   40
ʒett, to weir trapperis at the ʒuill,
I wald be spurrit at everie spald.
    Schir lat it nevir in toun be tald
    That I suld be ane ʒowllis ʒald!

Now lufferis cummis with larges lowd   45
Quhy sould not palfrayis thane be prowd,
Quhen gillettis wil be schomd and schroud
That ridden ar baith with lord and lawd?
    Schir lat it nevir in toun be tald
    That I suld be ane ʒowllis ʒald!   50

Quhen I was ʒoung and into ply
And wald cast gammaldis to the sky
I had beine bocht in realmes by
Had I consentit to be sauld;
    Schir lett it nevir in toun be tald   55
    That I suld be ane ʒowllis ʒald!

27 *dautit*, petted   30 *reiv wald*, would devour   34 *aucht*, property   35
soutteris, cobblers   36 *gumes*, gums   40 *forriddin*, over-ridden   41 *trapperis*,
trappings   42 *spald*, shoulder   45 *larges*, largesse, gifts   47 *gillettis*, mares;
schomd, groomed; *schroud*, decked out   48 *lawd*, serving man   51 *into ply*, in
good condition   52 *gammaldis*, capers

With gentill hors quhen I wald knyp
Thane is thair laid on me ane quhip,
To colleveris than man I skip
That scabbit ar, hes cruik and cald.   60
    Schir lett it nevir in toun be tald
    That I suld be ane ӡowllis ӡald!

Thocht in the stall I be not clappit
As cursouris that in silk beine trappit,
With ane new hous I wald be happit   65
Aganis this Crysthinmes for the cald;
    Schir lett it nevir in toun be tald
    That I suld be ane ӡowllis ӡald!

    Respontio Regis
Efter our wrettingis, thesaurer,
Tak in this gray hors, Auld Dumbar,   70
Quhilk in my aucht with service trew
In lyart changeit is in hew.
Gar hows him now aganis this ӡuill
And busk him lyk ane bischopis muill,
For with my hand I have indost   75
To pay quhatevir his trappouris cost.

57 *knyp*, graze   59 *colleveris*, coal-horses   60 *cruik*, bent, lameness   71 *aucht*, possession   72 *lyart*, grey-streaked   75 *indost*, endorsed

18. A BRASH OF WOWING

In secreit place this hyndir nycht
I hard ane beyrne say till ane bricht,
'My huny, my hart, my hoip, my heill,
I have bene lang 3our luifar leill
And can of 3ow get confort nane;   5
How lang will 3e with danger deill?
    3e brek my hart, my bony ane!'

His bony berd was kemmit and croppit,
Bot all with cale it was bedroppit,
And he wes townysche, peirt and gukit,   10
He clappit fast, he kist and chukkit,
As with the glaikis he wer ouirgane,
3it be his feirris he wald have fukkit;
    '3e brek my hart, my bony ane!'

Quod he, 'My hairt, sweit as the hunye,   15
Sen that I borne wes of my mynnye,
I never wowit weycht bot 3ow;
My wambe is of 3our luif sa fow,
That as ane gaist I glour and grane,
I trymble sa, 3e will not trow;   20
    3e brek my hart, my bony ane!'

'Tehe!' quod scho, and gaif ane gawfe,
'Be still my tuchan and my calfe,
My new spanit howffling fra the sowk,
And all the blythnes of my bowk,   25
My sweit swanking, saif 3ow allane
Na leyd I luiffit all this owk;
    Full leifis me your graceles gane.'

1 *hyndir*, recent   2 *beyrne*, fellow; *bricht*, pretty girl   9 *cale*, cabbage soup
10 *townysche*, cheaply smart; *gukit*, foolish   11 *clappit*, fondled; *chukkit*,
chucked under the chin   12 *glaikis*, desire   13 *feirris*, behaviour   18 *wambe*,
belly; *fow*, full   22 *gawfe*, guffaw   23 *tuchan*, stuffed calf-skin   24 *spanit*,
weaned; *howffling*, stupid fellow; *sowk*, milk   25 *bowk*, body   26 *swanking*,
smart young fellow   27 *leyd*, person; *owk*, week   28 *leifis me*, is dear to me;
gane, ugly mug

Quod he, 'My claver, and my curldodie,
My huny soppis, my sweit possodie,
Be not oure bosteous to зour billie,
Be warme hairtit and not ewill willie;
зour hals, quhyt as quhalis bane,
Garris ryis on loft my quhillelillie;
    зe brek my hart, my bony ane!'   35

Quod scho, 'My clype, my unspaynit gyane,
With moderis mylk зit in your mychane,
My belly huddrun, my swete hurle bawsy,
My huny gukkis, my slawsy gawsy,
зour musing waild perse ane harte of stane,   40
Tak gud confort, my grit heidit slawsy,
    Full leifis me your graceles gane.'

Quod he, 'My kyd, my capirculзoun,
My bony baib with the ruch brylзoun,
My tendir gyrle, my wallie gowdye,   45
My tyrlie myrlie, my crowdie mowdie;
Quhone that oure mouthis dois meit at ane
My stang dois storkyn with зour towdie;
    зe brek my hairt, my bony ane!'

Quod scho, 'Now tak me be the hand,   50
Welcum, my golk of Marie land,
My chirrie and my maikles munзoun,
My sowklar sweit as ony unзoun,
My strwmill stirk, зit new to spane,
I am applyit to your opunзoun;   55
    I luif rycht weill your graceles gane.'

29 *claver*, clover; *curldodie*, ribwort plantain   30 *possodie* , sheep's head broth
31 *billie*, lover   32 *ewill willie*, unkind   34 *quhillelillie*, penis   36 *clype*, silly
fellow; *unspaynit*, unweaned; *gyane*, giant   37 *mychane*, ?mouth   38 *huddrun*,
glutton; *hurle bawsy*, obscure term of endearment   39 *huny gukkis*, sweet fool;
slawsy gawsy, ?jolly sloven   43 *capirculзoun*, woodgrouse   44 *ruch brylзoun*,
hairy private parts   45 *wallie*, fine; *gowdye*, piece of gold   46 *tyrlie myrlie*,
crowdie mowdie, obscure (and probably obscene) terms of endearment   48
stang, penis; *towdie*, buttocks   51 *golk*, cuckoo   52 *maikles munзoun*, matchless
darling   53 *sowklar*, sucking child; *unзoun*, onion   54 *strwmill stirk*, ugly
young bullock   55 *applyit*, inclined

He gaiff to hir ane apill rubye;
Quod scho, 'Gramercye, my sweit cowhubye.'
And thai twa to ane play began,
Quhilk men dois call the dery dan   60
Quhill bayth thair bewis did meit in ane.
'Wo is me!' quod scho, 'quhair will ȝe, man?
    Best now I luif that graceles gane.'

19. OF A DANCE IN THE QUENIS CHALMER

Sir Jhon Sinclair begowthe to dance
For he was new cum owt of France;
For ony thing that he do mycht,
The ane futt 3eid ay onrycht
And to the tother wald not gree.   5
Quod ane, 'Tak up the Quenis knycht':
    A mirrear dance mycht na man see.

Than cam in Maistir Robert Scha,
He leuket as he culd lern tham a,
Bot ay his ane futt did waver,   10
He stackeret lyk ane strummall aver
That hopschackellt war aboin the kne,
To seik fra Sterling to Stranaver,
    A mirrear daunce mycht na man see.

Than cam in the Maister Almaser,   15
An hommiltye jommeltye juffler,
Lyk a stirk stackarand in the ry;
His hippis gaff mony hoddous cry.
John Bute the Fule said, 'Waes me!
He is bedirtin, fye! fy!'   20
    A mirrear dance mycht na man se.

Than cam in Dunbar the Mackar,
On all the flure thair was nane frackar;
And thair he dancet the dirrye dantoun,
He hoppet lyk a pillie wanton,   25
For luff of Musgraeffe, men tellis me;
He trippet quhill he tint his panton,
    A mirrear dance mycht na man se.

---

4 *onrycht*, wrong   11 *strummall aver*, gaunt old horse   12 *hopschackellt*,
hobbled   15 *almaser*, almoner   16 *hommiltye jommeltye juffler*, awkward
clown   20 *he is bedirtin*, he has fouled himself   23 *frackar*, more eager   24
dirrye dantoun, a lively dance   25 *pillie*, colt   27 *panton*, slipper

Than cam in maesteress Musgraeffe,
Scho mycht heff lernit all the laeffe; 30
Quhen I schau hir sa trimlye dance,
Hir guid convoy and contenance,
Than for hir saek I wissitt to be
The grytest erle or duk in France:
    A mirrear dance mycht na man see. 35

Than cam in Dame Dounteboir,
God waett gif that schou louket sowr;
Schou maid sic morgeownis with hir hippis,
For lachtter nain mycht hald thair lippis;
Quhen schou was danceand bisselye, 40
Ane blast of wind son fra hir slippis,
    A mirrear dance mycht na man see.

Quhen thair was cum in fyve or sax,
The Quenis dog begowthe to rax
And of his band he maid a bred 45
And to the danceing soin he him med;
Quhou mastevlyk about ʒeid he!
He stinckett lyk a tyk, sum said,
    A mirrear dance mycht na man se.

37 *waett*, knows   38 *morgeownis*, contortions   44 *rax*, stretch   45 *of his*
band... bred, from his leash he made a spring   48 *tyk*, cur

20. OF JAMES DOG, KEPAIR OF THE QUENIS WARDREP

The Wardraipper of Venus boure
To giff a doublett he is als doure
As it war off ane futt syd frog;
 Madame, ʒe heff a dangerous Dog!

Quhene that I schawe to him ʒour markis,   5
He turnis to me again and barkis
As he war wirriand ane hog:
 Madame, ʒe heff a dangerous Dog!

Quhen that I schawe to him ʒour wrytin
He girnis that I am red for bytin;   10
I wald he had ane havye clog:
 Madame, ʒe heff ane dangerous Dog!

Quhen that I speik till him freindlyk,
He barkis lyk ane midding tyk
War chassand cattell throu a bog: 15
 Madam, ʒe heff a dangerous Dog!

He is ane mastive, mekle of mycht,
To keip ʒour wardroippe ouer nycht
Fra the grytt Sowdan Gog-ma-gog:
 Madam, ʒe heff a dangerous Dog!   20

He is owre mekle to be ʒour messan,
Madame, I red ʒou get a less ane,
His gang garris all ʒour chalmeris schog,
 Madam, ʒe heff a dangerous Dog!

---

1 *wardraipper*, master of the wardrobe   3 *futt syd frog*, full-length cloak   5
markis, seal   10 *girnis*, snarls; *red for*, afraid of   14 *midding*, dunghill   21
messan, lapdog   22 *red*, advise   23 *gang*, walk; *schog*, shake

O Gracious Princes, guid and fair,
Do weill to James ȝour Wardraipair
Quhais faythfull bruder maist freind I am:
    He is na Dog, he is a Lam.

Thocht I in ballet did with him bourde,   5
In malice spack I nevir a woord
Bot all, my Dame, to do ȝou gam:
    He is na Dog, he is a Lam.

ȝour Hienes can nocht gett ane meter
To keip ȝour wardrope, nor discreter   10
To rewle ȝour robbis and dres the sam:
    He is na Dog, he is a Lam.

The wyff that he had in his innis,
That with the taingis wald braek his schinnis,
I wald schou drownet war in a dam: 15
    He is na Dog, he is a Lam.

The wyff that wald him kuckald mak,
I wald schou war, bayth syd and back,
Weill batteret with ane barrou tram:
    He is na Dog, he is an Lam.   20

He hes sa weill doin me obey
In till all thing, thairfoir I pray
That nevir dolour mak him dram:
    He is na Dog, he is a Lam.

5 *bourde*, jest   7 *do ȝou gam*, give you pleasure   13 *innis*, house   14 *taingis*,
tongs   19 *barrou tram*, shaft of a barrow   23 *dram*, sad

22. THE FEN3EIT FREIR OF TUNGLAND
(how he fell in the myre fleand to Turkiland)

As yung Awrora with cristall haile
In orient schew hir visage paile,
A swenyng swyth did me assaile
   Off sonis of Sathanis seid;
Me thocht a Turk of Tartary   5
Come throw the boundis of Barbary,
And lay forloppin in Lumbardy
   Full lang in waithman weid.

Fra baptasing for to eschew,
Thair a religious man he slew   10
And cled him in his abeit new,
   For he cowth wryte and reid.
Quhen kend was his dissimulance,
And all his cursit govirnance,
For feir he fled and come in France,   15
   With littill of Lumbard leid.

To be a leiche he fenyt him thair,
Quhilk mony a man micht rew evirmair,
For he left nowthir seik nor sair
   Unslane or he hyne 3eid.   20
Vane organis he full clenely carvit;
Quhen of his straik so mony starvit
Dreid he had gottin that he desarvit,
   He fled away gud speid.

In Scotland than the narrest way   25
He come, his cunnyng till assay;
To sum man thair it was no play
   The preving of his sciens.
In pottingry he wrocht grit pyne,
He murdreist mony in medecyne,   30
The jow was of a grit engyne,
   And generit was of gyans.

3 *swenying*, dream; *swyth*, at once   7 *forloppin*, renegade   8 *waithman*, outlaw
20 *hyne 3eid*, went hence   21 *vane organis*, jugular veins   22 *starvit*, died   29
pottingry, pharmacy   31 *jow*, jew, infidel

In leichecraft he was homecyd,
He wald haif, for a nicht to byd,
A haiknay and the hurt manis hyd,   35
   So meikle he was of myance.
His yrnis was rude as ony rawchtir,
Quhair he leit blude it was no lawchtir,
Full mony instrument for slawchtir
   Was in his gardevyance.   40

He cowth gif cure for laxatyve,
To gar a wicht hors want his lyve;
Quha evir assay wald, man or wyve,
   Thair hippis ʒeid hiddy giddy.
His practikis nevir war put to preif   45
But suddane deid or grit mischeif;
He had purgatioun to mak a theif
   To dee withowt a widdy.

Unto no mess pressit this prelat,
For sound of sacring bell nor skellat,   50
As blaksmyth bruikit was his pallatt
   For battering at the study.
Thocht he come hame a new maid channoun,
He had dispensit with matynnis channoun,
On him come nowther stole nor fannoun   55
   For smowking of the smydy.

Me thocht seir fassonis he assailʒeit
To mak the quintessance, and failʒeit,
And quhen he saw that nocht availʒeit,
   A fedrem on he tuke   60
And schupe in Turky for to fle,
And quhen that he did mont on he,
All fowill ferleit quhat he sowld be,
   That evir did on him luke.

35 *haiknay*, riding horse   36 *myance*, resource   37 *yrnis*, surgical instruments;
rawchtir, rafter   40 *gardevyance*, chest   42 *wicht*, strong   44 *hiddy giddy*, all
over the place   48 *widdy*, noose   50 *skellat*, handbell   51 *bruikit*, blackened;
pallatt, pate   53 *channoun*, canon   54 *channoun*, canonical   55 *fannoun*, an
ecclesiastical vestment   57 *seir*, many; *fassonis*, fashions   60 *fedrem*, coat of
feathers   63 *ferleit*, marvelled

Sum held he had bene Dedalus, 65
Sum the Menatair marvelus,
Sum Martis blaksmyth Vulcanus,
    And sum Saturnus kuke.
And evir the cuschettis at him tuggit,
The rukis him rent, the ravynis him druggit, 70
The hudit crawis his hair furth ruggit,
    The hevin he micht not bruke.

The myttane and Sanct Martynis fowle
Wend he had bene the hornit howle,
Thay set aupone him with a ȝowle 75
    And gaif him dynt for dynt.
The golk, the gormaw and the gled,
Beft him with buffettis quhill he bled;
The sparhalk to the spring him sped,
    Als fers as fyre of flynt. 80

The tarsall gaif him tug for tug,
A stanchell hang in ilka lug,
The pyot furth his pennis did rug,
    The stork straik ay but stynt;
The bissart, bissy but rebuik, 85
Scho was so cleverus of hir cluik,
His bawis he micht not langer bruik,
    Scho held thame at ane hint.

Thik was the clud of kayis and crawis,
Of marleȝonis, mittanis, and of mawis, 90
That bikkrit at his berd with blawis
    In battell him abowt.
Thay nybbillit him with noyis and cry,
The rerd of thame rais to the sky,
And evir he cryit on Fortoun, Fy! 95
    His lyfe was in to dowt.

68 *kuke*, cook   69 *cuschettis*, doves   70 *druggit*, tore at   71 *ruggit*, pulled
72 *bruke*, enjoy   73 *myttane*, bird of prey; *Sanct Martynis fowle*, hen harrier 74
hornit howle, long-eared owl   76 *dynt*, blow   77 *golk*, cuckoo; *gormaw*,
cormorant; *gled*, kite   79 *spring*, attack   81 *tarsall*, peregrine falcon 82
stanchell, kestrel   83 *pyot*, magpie; *pennis*, feathers   84 *stynt*, pause 85
bissart, buzzard; *but rebuik*, without pause   86 *cleverus*, nimble; *cluik*, claws
87 *bawis*, balls   88 *hint*, grip   89 *kayis*, jackdaws   90 *marleȝonis*, merlins;
mittanis, v. line 73; *mawis*, gulls   94 *rerd*, noise

54

The ja him skrippit with a skryke
And skornit him as it was lyk;
The egill strong at him did stryke
    And rawcht him mony a rowt.   100
For feir uncunnandly he cawkit
Quhill all his pennis war drownd and drawkit,
He maid a hundreth nolt all hawkit
    Beneth him with a spowt.

He schewre his feddreme that was schene,   105
And slippit owt of it full clene,
And in a myre, up to the ene,
    Amang the glar did glyd.
The fowlis all at the fedrem dang,
As at a monster thame amang,   110
Quhill all the pennis of it owsprang
    In till the air full wyde.

And he lay at the plunge evirmair
So lang as any ravin did rair,
The crawis him socht with cryis of cair   115
    In every schaw besyde.
Had he reveild bene to the ruikis,
Thay had him revin all with thair cluikis:
Thre dayis in dub amang the dukis
    He did with dirt him hyde.   120

The air was dirkit with the fowlis,
That come with ȝawmeris and with ȝowlis,
With skryking, skrymming, and with scowlis,
    To tak him in the tyde.
I walknit with the noyis and schowte,   125
So hiddowis beir was me abowte;
Sensyne I curs that cankerit rowte,
    Quhair evir I go or ryde.

97 *skrippit*, mocked; *skryke*, screech   100 *rowt*, blow   101 *uncunnandly*,
clumsily; *cawkit*, shat   102 *drawkit*, drenched   103 *nolt*, cattle; *hawkit*,
streaked   105 *schewre*, displayed; *feddreme*, v. line 60   108 *glar*, mud   111
owsprang, sprang out   113 *plunge*, deep pool   114 *ravin*, raven   116 *schaw*,
thicket   119 *dub*, stagnant pool; *dukis*, ducks   126 *beir*, din   127 *sensyne*,
since then

I, Maister Andro Kennedy,
   Curro quando sum vocatus,
Gottin with sum incuby,
   Or with sum freir *infatuatus;*
In faith I can nought tell redly,   5
   Unde aut ubi fui natus,
Bot in treuth I trow trewly,
   Quod sum diabolus incarnatus.

Cum nihil sit certius morte,
   We mon all de, quhen we haif done,   10
Nescimus quando vel qua sorte,
   Na blind Allane wait of the mone,
Ego patior in pectore,
   This night I mycht not sleip a wink;
Licet eger in corpore,   15
   ȝit wald my mouth be wet with drink.

Nunc condo testamentum meum,
   I leiff my saull for evirmare,
Per omnipotentem Deum,
   In to my lordis wyne cellar;   20
Semper ibi ad ramanendum,
   Quhill domisday without dissever,
Bonum vinum ad bibendum,
   With sueit Cuthbert that lufit me nevir.

Ipse est dulcis ad amandum,   25
   He wald oft ban me in his breith,
Det michi modo at potandum,
   And I forgif him laith and wraith:
Quia in cellario cum cervicia,
   I had lever lye baith air and lait,   30
Nudus solus in camesia,
   Na in my Lordis bed of stait.

26 *ban,* curse   28 *laith and wraith,* harm and anger   30 *air,* early

A barrell bung ay at my bosum,
   Of warldis gud I had na mair;
Corpus meum ebriosum   35
   I leif on to the toun of Air;
In a draf midding for ever and ay
   Ut ibi sepeliri queam,
Quhair drink and draff may ilka day
   Be cassyne *super faciem meam.*   40

I leif my hert that never wes sicir,
   Sed semper variabile,
That nevir mair wald flow and flicir,
   Consorti meo Iacobe:
Thocht I wald bynd it with a wicir,   45
   Verum Deum renui;
Bot and I hecht to teme a bicker,
   Hoc pactum semper tenui.

Syne leif I the best aucht I bocht,
   Quod est Latinum propter caupe,   50
To hede of my kyn, bot I wait nocht
   Quis est ille, than schrew my skawpe:
I callit my Lord my heid, but hiddill,
   Sed nulli alii hoc dixerunt,
We weir als sib as seve and riddill,   55
   In una silva que creverunt.

Omnia mea solacia,
   Thay wer bot lesingis all and ane,
Cum omni fraude et fallacia
   I leif the maister of Sanct Antane,   60
Willilmo Gray, *sine gratia,*
   My awin deir cusing, as I wene,
Qui nunquam fabricat mendacia,
   Bot quhen the holyne growis grene.

---

37 *draf midding* a heap of the refuse from brewing   39 *draff,* the dregs of malt
40 *cassyne,* thrown   47 *teme a bicker,* empty a beaker   49 *aucht,* possession
52 *schrew my skawpe,* curse my head   53 *hiddill,* secrecy   55 *seve and riddill,*
sieve and riddle   58 *lesingis,* lies   64 *holyne,* holly

My fenȝeing and my fals wynyng 65
  Relinquo falsis fratribus;
For that is Goddis awin bidding,
  Dispersit dedit pauperibus.
For menis saulis thai say and sing,
  Mentientes pro muneribus; 70
Now God gif thame ane evil ending,
  Pro suis pravis operibus.

To Iok Fule, my foly fre
  Lego post corpus sepultum;
In faith I am mair fule than he, 75
  Licet ostendo bonum vultum:
Of corne and catall, gold and fe,
  Ipse habet valde multum,
And ȝit he bleris my lordis E
  Fingendo eum fore stultum. 80

To Maister Johne Clerk syne,
  Do et lego intime,
Goddis malisone and myne,
  Ipse est causa mortis mee.
War I a dog and he a swyne, 85
  Multi mirantur super me,
Bot I suld gar that lurdane quhryne,
  Scribendo dentes sine de.

Residuum omnium bonorum
  For to dispone my Lord sall haif, 90
Cum tutela puerorum,
  Ade, Kytte, and all the laif.
In faith I will no langar raif:
  Pro sepultura ordino
On the new gys, sa God me saif, 95
  Non sicut more solito.

---

65 *wynyng,* whining   87 *lurdane,* lazy fellow   93 *raif,* rave

In die mee sepulture
   I will nane haif bot our awne gyng,
Et duos rusticos de rure
   Berand a barell on a styng;   100
Drynkand and playand cop out evin,
   Sicut egomet solebam;
Singand and gretand with hie stevin,
   Potum meum cum fletu miscebam.

I will na preistis for me sing,   105
   Dies illa, Dies ire;
Na ȝit na bellis for me ring,
   Sicut semper solet fieri;
Bot a bagpipe to play a spryng,
   Et unum ailwosp *ante me;*   110
In stayd of baners for to bring
   Quatuor lagenas cervicie,
Within the graif to set sic thing,
   In modum crucis juxta me,
To fle the fendis, than hardely sing   115
   De terra plasmasti me.

98 *gyng*, gang, company   100 *styng*, pole   101 *cop out evin*, draining the cup
103 *gretand*, weeping; *hie stevin*, loudly   110 *ailwosp*, a wisp of hay, sign of an
alehouse

We that ar heir in hevins glory,
To ȝow that ar in purgatory,
Commendis us on our hairtly wyis;
I mene we folk in parradyis,
In Edinburgh with all mirrines,   5
To ȝow of Strivilling in distres,
Quhair nowdir plesance nor delyt is,
For pety this epistell wrytis.
O! ȝe heremeitis and hankersaidilis,
That takis ȝour pennance at ȝour tablis,   10
And eitis nocht meit restorative,
Nor drynkis no wyn confortative,
Bot aill and that is thyn and small,
With few coursis into ȝour hall,
But cumpany of lordis and knychtis,   15
Or ony uder gudly wichtis,
Solitar, walkand ȝour allone,
Seing no thing bot stok and stone;
Out of ȝour panefull purgatory,
To bring ȝow to the blis of glory   20
Off Edinburgh, the mirry toun,
We sall begyn ane cairfull soun,
Ane dergy devoit and meik,
The Lord of blis doing beseik
ȝow to delyver out of ȝour noy,   25
And bring ȝow sone to Edinburgh joy,
For to be mirry amang us;
And sa the dergy begynis thus.

Lectio prima
The Fader, the Sone, and Haly Gaist,
The mirthfull Mary, virgene chaist,   30
Of Angellis all the ordouris nyne,
And all the hevinly court devyne,
Sone bring ȝow fra the pyne and wo
Of Strivilling, every court manis fo,
Agane to Edinburghis joy and blis,   35
Quhair wirschep, welth, and weilfar is,
Pley, plesance, and eik honesty:
Say ȝe amen for cheritie.

9 *hankersaidilis*, anchorets

Responsio, Tu autem, Domine

Tak consolatioun	In ȝour pane,	
In tribulatioun	Tak consolatioun,	40
Out of vexatioun	Cum hame agane,	
Tak consolatioun	In ȝour pane.	

Jube Domine benedicere

Oute of distres of Strivilling toun
To Edinburch blis God mak ȝow boun.

Lectio secunda

Patriarchis, profeitis, and appostillis deir,   45
Confessouris, virgynis, and marteris cleir,
And all the saitt celestiall,
Devotely we upoun thame call,
That sone out of ȝour panis fell,
ȝe may in hevin heir with us dwell,   50
To eit swan, cran, pertrik, and plever,
And every fische that swymis in rever;
To drynk with us the new fresche wyne,
That grew upoun the rever of ryne,
Fresche fragrant clairettis out of France,   55
Of Angers and of Orliance,
With mony ane cours of grit dyntie:
Say ȝe amen for cheritie.

Responsorium, Tu autem Domine

God and Sanct Jeill	Heir ȝow convoy	
Baith sone and weill,	God and Sanct Jeill	60
To sonce and seill,	Solace and joy,	
God and Sanct Geill	Hier ȝow convoy.	

Jube Domine benedicere

Out of Strivilling panis fell,
In Edinburch joy sone mot ȝe dwell.

---

44 *boun*, ready to go   47 *saitt*, assembly   51 *cran*, crane   61 *sonce and seill*, plenty and happiness

We pray to all the Sanctis of hevin   65
That ar aboif the sterris sevin
ȝow to deliver out of your pennance
That ȝe may sone play, sing and dance
Heir in to Edinburch and mak gude cheir
Quhair welth and weilfair is but weir;   70
And I that dois ȝour panis discryve
Thinkis for to vissy ȝow belyve;
Nocht in desert with ȝow to dwell
Bot as the angell Sanct Gabriell
Dois go betwene fra hevinis glory   75
To thame that ar in purgatory,
And in thair tribulatioun
To gif thame consolatioun,
And schaw thame quhen thair panis ar past
They sall till hevin cum at last,   80
And how nane servis to haif sweitnes
That nevir taistit bittirnes;
And thairfoir how suld ȝe considdir
Of Edinburgh bliss quhen ȝe cum hiddir
Bot gif ȝe taistit had befoir   85
Of Strivilling toun the panis soir.
And thairfoir tak in patience
ȝour pennance and ȝour abstinence,
And ȝe sall cum, or ȝule begyn,
Into the bliss that we ar in;   90
Quhilk grant the glorius Trinitie!
Say ȝe amen for cheritie.

Responsorium

Cum hame and dwell	No moir in Strivilling,
Frome hiddous hell	Cum hame and dwell,
Quhair fische to sell	Is non bot spirling; 95
Cam hame and dwell	No moir in Strivilling.

---

70 *but weir*, certainly   72 *vissy*, visit; *belyve*, at once   81 *servis*, deserves   95
spirling, smelts

Et ne nos inducas in temptationem de Strivilling:
Sed libera nos a malo illius.
Requiem Edinburgi dona eiis, Domine,
Et lux ipsius luceat eiis. 100
A porta tristicie de Strivilling,
Erue, Domine, animas et corpora eorum.
Credo gustare statim vinum Edinburgi,
In villa viventium.
Requiescant Edinburgi. Amen. 105

Deus qui iustos et corde humiles Ex omni eorum tribulatione liberare
dignatus es, Libera famulos tuos apud villam de Stirling versantes A
penis et tristitiis eiusdem, Et ad Edinburgi gaudia eos perducas, Ut
requiescat Strivilling. Amen

Quhy will 3e, merchantis of renoun,
Lat Edinburgh, 3our nobill toun,
For laik of reformatioun
The commone proffeitt tyine and fame?
   Think 3e not schame,   5
That onie uther regioun
Sall with dishonour hurt 3our name?

May nane pas throw 3our principall gaittis
For stink of haddockis and of scaittis,
For cryis of carlingis and debaittis,   10
For fensum flyttingis of defame:
   Think 3e not schame,
Befoir strangeris of all estaittis
That sic dishonour hurt 3our name?

3our stinkand scull, that standis dirk,   15
Haldis the lycht fra 3our parroche kirk;
Your foirstair makis 3our housis mirk,
Lyk na cuntray bot heir at hame:
   Think 3e not schame,
Sa litill polesie to wirk   20
In hurt and sklander of 3our name?

At 3our hie Croce, quhar gold and silk
Sould be, thair is bot crudis and milk;
And at 3our Trone bot cokill and wilk,
Pansches, pudingis of Jok and Jame: 25
   Think 3e not schame,
Sen as the world sayis that ilk
In hurt and sclander of 3our name?

---

4 *tyine*, lose   8 *gaittis*, streets   10 *carlingis*, old women   11 *fensum*, offensive
20 *polesie*, improvement   23 *crudis*, curds   25 *pansches*, tripes   27 *that ilk*,
the same thing

Your commone menstrallis hes no tone
Bot 'Now the day dawis', and 'Into Joun';   30
Cunningar men man serve Sanct Cloun,
And nevir to uther craftis clame:
    Think ȝe not schame,
To hald sic mowaris on the moyne,
In hurt and sclander of ȝour name?   35

Tailȝouris, soutteris, and craftis vyll,
The fairest of ȝour streittis dois fyll;
And merchandis at the stinkand styll
Ar hamperit in ane hony came:
    Think ȝe not schame,   40
That ȝe have nether witt nor wyll
To win ȝourselff ane bettir name?

ȝour burgh of beggeris is ane nest,
To schout thai swentȝouris will not rest;
All honest folk they do molest,   45
Sa piteuslie thai cry and rame:
    Think ȝe not schame,
That for the poore hes nothing drest,
In hurt and sclander of ȝour name?

ȝour proffeit daylie dois incres,   50
ȝour godlie workis les and les;
Through streittis nane may mak progres
For cry of cruikit, blind, and lame:
    Think ȝe not schame,
That ȝe sic substance dois posses,   55
And will nocht win ane bettir name?

Sen for the Court and the Sessioun,
The great repair of this regioun
Is in ȝour burgh, thairfoir be boun
To mend all faultis that ar to blame,   60
    And eschew schame;
Gif thai pas to ane uther toun
ȝe will decay, and ȝour great name.

29 *tone*, tune   34 *mowaris*, mockers; *moyne*, moon   36 *soutteris*, cobblers
39 *hamperit*, cramped; *hony came*, honeycomb   44 *swentȝouris*, vagabonds
46 *rame*, shout   59 *boun*, ready

65

Thairfoir strangeris and liegis treit,
Tak not ouer meikle for thair meit,   65
And gar ʒour merchandis be discreit,
That na extortiounes be, proclame
    All fraud and schame:
Keip ordour, and poore nighbouris beit,
That ʒe may gett ane bettir name!   70

Singular proffeit so dois ʒow blind,
The common proffeit gois behind:
I pray that Lord remeid to fynd,
That deit into Jerusalem,
    And gar ʒou schame!   75
That sum tyme ressoun may ʒow bind,
For to [   ] ʒow guid name.

64 *treit*, treat well, entertain   69 *beit*, relieve

26. THE TWA CUMMERIS

Rycht airlie on Ask Weddinsday
Drynkand the wyne satt cumeris tway;
The tane cowth to the tother complene,
Graneand and suppand cowd scho say,
'This lang Lentern makis me lene.'   5

On cowch besyd the fyre scho satt,
God wait gif scho wes grit and fatt,
ʒit to be feble scho did hir fene
And ay scho said, 'Latt preif of that,
This lang Lentern makis me lene.'   10

'My fair sweit cummer,' quod the tuder,
'ʒe tak that nigertnes of ʒour muder;
All wyne to test scho wald disdane
Bot mavasy, scho bad nane uder;
This lang Lentern makis me lene.'   15

'Cummer, be glaid both evin and morrow,
Thocht ʒe suld bayth beg and borrow,
Fra our lang fasting ʒe ʒow refrene,
And latt ʒour husband dre the sorrow;
This lang Lentern makis me lene.'   20

'ʒour counsale, cummer, is gud,' quod scho,
'All is to tene him that I do,
In bed he is nocht wirth a bene;
Fill fow the glass and drynk me to;
This lang Lentern makis me lene.'   25

Off wyne owt of ane choppyne stowp,
They drank two quartis, sowp and sowp,
Off drowth sic exces did thame strene;
Be than to mend thay had gud howp.
'This lang Lentroun makis me lene.'   30

2 *cumeris*, gossips   4 *graneand*, groaning   9 *latt preif of*, let me taste   12
nigertnes, niggardliness   19 *dre*, endure   22 *tene*, annoy   26 *choppyne stowp*,
Scots half-pint measure   27 *sowp and sowp*, turn about   28 *drowth*, thirst;
strene, distress

67

Apon the Midsummer evin, mirriest of nichtis,
I muvit furth allane, neir as midnicht wes past,
Besyd ane gudlie grein garth, full of gay flouris,
Hegeit of ane huge hicht with hawthorne treis
Quhairon ane bird on ane bransche so birst out hir notis   5
That never ane blythfullar bird was on the beuche hard:
Quhat throw the sugarat sound of hir sang glaid,
And throw the savour sanative of the sueit flouris,
I drew in derne to the dyk to dirkin efter mirthis;
The dew donkit the daill and dynnit the feulis.   10
I hard, under ane holyn hevinlie grein hewit,
Ane hie speiche, at my hand, with hautand wourdis;
With that in haist to the hege so hard I inthrang
That I was heildit with hawthorne and with heynd leveis:
Throw pykis of the plet thorne I presandlie luikit,   15
Gif ony persoun wald approche within that plesand garding.
I saw thre ladeis sit in ane grein arbeir,
All grathit in to garlandis of fresche gudlie flouris;
So glitterit as the gold wer thair glorius gilt tressis,
Quhill all the gressis did gleme of the glaid hewis;   20
Kemmit war thair cleir hair, and curiouslie sched
Attour thair schulderis doun schyre, schyning full bricht;
With curches, cassin thair abone, of kirsp cleir and thin:
Thair mantillis grein war as the gress that grew in May sessoun,
Fetrit with thair quhyt fingaris about thair fair sydis: 25
Off ferlifull fyne favour was thair faceis meik,
All full of flurist fairheid, as flouris in June;
Quhyt, seimlie, and soft, as the sweit lillies
New upspred upon spray, as new spynist rose;
Arrayit ryallie about with mony rich vardour,   30
That nature full nobillie annamalit with flouris
Off alkin hewis under hevin, that ony heynd knew,

---

6 *beuche*, branch   8 *sanative*, healing   9 *derne*, darkness; *dirkin*, lurk; *mirthis*,
entertainment   10 *donkit*, dampened   12 *hautand*, haughty   13 *inthrang*,
pushed in   14 *heildit*, hidden; *heynd*, pleasant   15 *plet*, interlaced   18
grathit, arrayed   21 *kemmit*, combed; *sched*, parted   22 *schyre*, shining   23
curches, woman's headdress, sometimes expensive and jewelled; *cassin*, thrown;
kirsp, gauze   25 *fetrit*, fastened   26 *ferlifull*, wonderful   30 *vardour*, greenery
32 *alkin*, every kind; *heynd*, gentle person

Fragrant, all full of fresche odour fynest of smell.
Ane cumlie tabil coverit wes befoir tha cleir ladeis,
With ryalle cowpis apon rawis full of ryche wynis.   35
And of thir fair wlonkes, tua weddit war with lordis,
Ane wes ane wedow, I wis, wantoun of laitis.
And, as thai talk at the tabill of many taill sindry,
Thay wauchtit at the wicht wyne and waris out wourdis;
And syn thai spak more spedelie, and sparit no matiris.   40
   Bewrie, said the Wedo, 3e woddit wemen 3ing,
Quhat mirth 3e fand in maryage, sen 3e war menis wyffis;
Reveill gif 3e rewit that rakles conditioun
Or gif that ever 3e luffit leyd upone lyf mair
Nor thame that 3e 3our fayth hes festinit for ever?   45
Or gif 3e think, had 3e chois, that 3e wald cheis better?
Think 3e it nocht ane blist band that bindis so fast,
That none undo it a deill may bot the deith ane?
   Than spak ane lusty belyf with lustie effeiris;
It, that 3e call the blist band that bindis so fast,   50
Is bair of blis and bailfull and greit barrat wirkis.
3e speir, had I fre chois, gif I wald cheis better?
Chen3eis ay ar to eschew; and changeis ar sueit:
Sic cursit chance till eschew, had I my chois anis,
Out of the chein3eis of ane churle I chaip suld for evir.   55
God gif matrimony were made to mell for ane 3eir!
It war bot merrens to be mair, bot gif our myndis pleisit:
It is agane the law of luf, of kynd, and of nature,
Togiddir hartis to strene, that stryveis with uther:
Birdis hes ane better law na bernis be meikill,   60
That ilk 3eir, with new joy, joyis ane maik,
And fangis thame ane fresche feyr, unful3eit, and constant,
And lattis thair ful3eit feiris flie quhair thai pleis.
Cryst gif sic ane consuetude war in this kith haldin!
Than weill war us wemen that ever we war fre;   65
We suld have feiris as fresche to fang quhen us likit,

---

35 *apon rawis*, in rows   36 *wlonkes*, ladies   37 *laitis*, manners   39 *wauchtit*,
quaffed; *wicht*, strong; *waris*, spent   41 *bewrie*, reveal   43 *rewit*, regretted
44 *leyd*, man   48 *bot the deith ane*, but death alone   49 *belyf*, at once; *effeiris*,
behaviour   51 *barrat*, trouble   53 *chen3eis*, chains   56 *mell*, involve oneself
57 *merrens*, vexation   60 *na bernis*, than men   61 *maik*, mate   62 *fangis*,
takes; *feyr*, mate; *unful3eit*, not exhausted   64 *kith*, country

And gif all larbaris thair leveis, quhen thai lak curage.
My self suld be full semlie in silkis arrayit,
Gymp, jolie, and gent, richt joyus, and gent.
I suld at fairis be found, new faceis to se;   70
At playis, and at preichingis, and pilgrimages greit,
To schaw my renone, royaly, quhair preis was of folk,
To manifest my makdome to multitude of pepill,
And blaw my bewtie on breid, quhair bernis war mony;
That I micht cheis, and be chosin, and change quhen me lykit. 75
Than suld I waill ane full weill, our all the wyd realme,
That suld my womanheid weild the lang winter nicht;
And when I gottin had ane grome, ganest of uther,
ʒaip, and ʒing, in the ʒok ane ʒeir for to draw;
Fra I had preveit his pitht the first plesand moneth,   80
Than suld I cast me to keik in kirk, and in markat,
And all the cuntre about, kyngis court, and uther,
Quhair I ane galland micht get aganis the nixt ʒeir,
For to perfurneis furth the werk quhen failʒeit the tother;
A forky fure, ay furthwart, and forsy in draucht,   85
Nother febill, nor fant, nor fulʒeit in labour,
But als fresche of his forme as flouris in May;
For all the fruit suld I fang, thocht he the flour burgeoun.
    I have ane wallidrag, ane worme, ane auld wobat carle,
A waistit wolroun, na worth bot wourdis to clatter;   90
Ane bumbart, ane dron bee, ane bag full of flewme,
Ane skabbit skarth, ane scorpioun, ane scutarde behind;
To see him scart his awin skyn grit scunner I think.
Quhen kissis me that carybald, than kyndillis all my sorow;
As birs of ane brym bair, his berd is als stif,   95
Bot soft and soupill as the silk is his sary lume;
He may weill to the syn assent, bot sakles is his deidis.
With gor is his tua grym ene ar gladderit all about,
And gorgeit luyk tua gutaris that war with glar stoppit;
Bot quhen that glowrand gaist grippis me about,   100

67 *larbaris*, impotent men   69 *gymp*, slender; *gent*, elegant   72 *preis*, crowd
73 *makdome*, comeliness   74 *on breid*, abroad   76 *waill*, choose   78 *grome*,
fellow; *ganest*, fittest   79 *ʒaip*, nimble   84 *perfurneis*, perform   85 *forky fure*,
?bold in the furrow; *forsy*, forceful   88 *fang*, take   89 *wallidrag*, slob; *wobat*,
caterpillar   90 *wolroun*, wild boar   91 *bumbart*, sluggard   92 *skarth*,
monster; *scutarde*, incontinent   93 *scart*, scratch; *scunner*, disgust   94 *carybald*,
cannibal   95 *birs*, bristles; *brym*, furious   96 *lume*, penis   97 *sakles*, sinless
98 *gor*, slime; *gladderit*, smeared   99 *glar*, mud

Than think I hiddowus Mahowne hes me in armes;
Thair ma na sanyne me save fra that auld Sathane;
For, thocht I croce me all cleine, fra the croun doun,
He wil my corse all beclip, and clap me to his breist.
Quhen schaiffyne is that ald schaik with a scharp rasour,   105
He schowis one me his schevill mouth and schedis my lippis;
And with his hard hurcheone scyne sa heklis he my chekis,
That as a glemand gleyd glowis my chaftis;
I schrenk for the scharp stound, bot schout dar I nought,
For schore of that auld schrew, schame him betide!   110
The luf blenkis of that bogill, fra his blerde ene,
As Belȝebub had one me blent, abasit my spreit;
And quhen the smy one me smyrkis with his smake smolet,
He fepillis like a farcy aver that flyrit one a gillot.
Quhen that the sound of his saw sinkis in my eris,   115
Than ay renewis my noy, or he be neir cumand:
Quhen I heir nemmyt his name, than mak I nyne crocis,
To keip me fra the cummerans of that carll mangit,
That full of eldnyng is and anger and all evill thewis.
I dar nought luke to my luf for that lene gib,   120
He is sa full of jelusy and engyne fals;
Ever ymagynyng in mynd materis of evill,
Compasand and castand casis a thousand
How he sall tak me, with a trawe, at trist of ane othir:
I dar nought keik to the knaip that the cop fillis,   125
For eldnyng of that ald schrew that ever one evill thynkis;
For he is waistit and worne fra Venus werkis,
And may nought beit worth a bene in bed of my mystirs.
He trowis that ȝoung folk I ȝerne ȝeild, for he gane is,
Bot I may ȝuke all this ȝer, or his ȝerd help.   130
    Ay quhen that caribald carll wald clyme one my wambe,
Than am I dangerus and daine and dour of my will;
ȝit leit I never that larbar my leggis ga betueene,

102 *sanyne*, cross oneself   105 *schaiffyne*, shaved; *schaik*, fellow   106 *schevill*,
twisted; *schedis*, parts   107 *hurcheone*, hedgehog; *scyne*, skin   108 *gleyd*, live
coal; *chaftis*, jaws   109 *stound*, pain   110 *schore*, menace   113 *smy*,
scoundrel; *smake smolet*, villainous muzzle   114 *fepillis*, put out lower lip; *farcy
aver*, diseased carthorse; *flyrit*, leers; *gillot*, mare   115 *saw*, talk   118 *mangit*,
crazed   119 *eldnyng*, jealousy; *thewis*, habits   124 *trawe*, trick   125 *knaip*,
manservant   128 *beit ... mystirs*, satisfy my lust   129 *ȝerne ȝeild*, eagerly pay;
gane, impotent   130 *ȝuke*, itch; *ȝerd*, penis   132 *dangerus*, reluctant; *daine*,
reserved   133 *larbar*, impotent fellow

71

To fyle my flesche, na fumyll me, without a fee gret;
And thoght his pene purly me payis in bed,   135
His purse pays richely in recompense efter:
For, or he clym on my corse, that carybald forlane,
I have conditioun of a curche of kersp all ther fynest,
A goun of engranyt claith, right gaily furrit,
A ring with a ryall stane, or other riche jowell,   140
Or rest of his rousty raid, thoght he wer rede wod:
For all the buddis of Johne Blunt, quhen he abone clymis,
Me think the baid deir aboucht, sa bawch ar his werkis;
And thus I sell him solace, thoght I it sour think:
Fra sic a syre, God ʒow saif, my sueit sisteris deir!   145
    Quhen that the semely had said her sentence to end,
Than all thai leuch apon loft with latis full mery,
And raucht the cop round about full of riche wynis,
And ralʒeit lang, or thai wald rest, with ryatus speche.
    The wedo [to] the tothir wlonk warpit ther wordis;   150
Now, fair sister, fallis ʒow but fenʒeing to tell,
Sen man ferst with matrimony ʒow menskit in kirk,
How haif ʒe farne be ʒour faith? confese us the treuth:
That band to blise, or to ban, quhilk ʒow best thinkis?
Or how ʒe like lif to leid in to lell spousage?   155
And syne my self ʒe exeme one the samyn wise,
And I sall say furth the south, dissymyland no word.
    The plesand said, I protest, the treuth gif I schaw,
That of ʒour toungis ʒe be traist. The tothir twa grantit;
With that sprang up hir spreit be a span hechar.   160
To speik, quoth scho, I sall nought spar; ther is no spy neir:
I sall a ragment reveil fra rute of my hert,
A roust that is sa rankild quhill risis my stomok;
Now sall the byle all out brist, that beild has so lang;
For it to beir one my breist wes berdin our hevy: 165
I sall the venome devoid with a vent large,
And me assuage of the swalme, that suellit wes gret.
    My husband wes a hur maister, the hugeast in erd,
Tharfor I hait him with my hert, sa help me our Lord!

135 *pene*, penis   137 *forlane*, despicable   139 *engranyt*, dyed in cochineal
141 *rede wod*, raving mad   142 *buddis*, bribes   143 *baid*, delay; *bawch*, feeble
147 *latis*, manners   149 *ralʒeit*, jested   150 *warpit*, addressed   152 *menskit*,
favoured   155 *lell*, faithful   156 *exeme*, examine   159 *traist*, secret   160
hechar, higher   163 *roust*, rancour   164 *beild*, swollen   167 *swalme*, swelling

He is a ʒoung man ryght ʒaip, bot nought in ʒouth flouris;   170
For he is fadit full far and feblit of strenth:
He wes as flurising fresche within this few ʒeris,
Bot he is falʒeid full far and fulʒeid in labour;
He has bene lychour so lang quhill lost is his natur,
His lume is waxit larbar, and lyis in to swonne: 175
Wes never sugeorne wer set na one that snaill tyrit,
For efter vii oulkis rest, it will nought rap anys;
He has bene waistit apone wemen, or he me wif chesit,
And in adultre, in my tyme, I haif him tane oft:
And ʒit he is als brankand with bonet one syde,   180
And blenkand to the brichtest that in the burgh duellis,
Alse curtly of his clething and kemmyng of his hair,
As he that is mare valʒeand in Venus chalmer;
He semys to be sumthing worth, that syphyr in bour,
He lukis as he wald luffit be, thocht he be litill of valour;   185
He dois as dotit dog that damys on all bussis,
And liftis his leg apone loft, thoght he nought list pische;
He has a luke without lust and lif without curage;
He has a forme without force and fessoun but vertu,
And fair wordis but effect, all fruster of dedis;   190
He is for ladyis in luf a right lusty schadow,
Bot in to derne, at the deid, he salbe drup fundin;
He ralis, and makis repet with ryatus wordis,
Ay rusing him of his radis and rageing in chalmer;
Bot God wait quhat I think quhen he so thra spekis,   195
And how it settis him so syde to sege of sic materis.
Bot gif him self, of sum evin, myght ane say amang thaim,
Bot he nought ane is, bot nane, of naturis possessoris.
Scho that has ane auld man nought all is begylit;
He is at Venus werkis na war na he semys: 200
I wend I josit a gem, and I haif geit gottin;
He had the glemying of gold, and wes bot glase fundin.
Thought men be ferse, wele I fynd, fra falʒe ther curage,
Thar is bot eldnyng or anger ther hertis within.
Ye speik of berdis one bewch: of blise may thai sing,   205

170 ʒaip, nimble   173 falʒeid, enfeebled; fulʒeid, worn out   176 sugeorne, rest
180 brankand, prancing   184 syphyr, cipher   186 damys, pisses   188 luke,
gaze   189 fessoun, appearance   192 drup, feeble   194 rusing, boasting; radis,
escapades   195 thra, wildly   196 syde, boastfully   201 I wend I josit, I
thought I had; geit, jet   203 fra falʒe ther curage, when their desire fails

73

That, one Sanct Valentynis day, ar vacandis ilk ȝer;
Hed I that plesand prevelege to part quhen me likit,
To change, and ay to cheise agane, than, chastite, adew!
Than suld I haif a fresch feir to fang in mynn armes:
To hald a freke, quhill he faynt, may foly be calit.   210
  Apone sic materis I mus, at mydnyght, full oft,
And murnys so in my mynd I murdris my selfin;
Than ly I walkand for wa, and walteris about,
Wariand oft my wekit kyn, that me away cast
To sic a craudoune but curage, that knyt my cler bewte,   215
And ther so mony kene knyghtis this kenrik within:
Than think I on a semelyar, the suth for to tell,
Na is our syre be sic sevin; with that I sych oft:
Than he ful tenderly dois turne to me his tume person,
And with a ȝoldin ȝerd dois ȝolk me in armys,   220
Amd sais, 'My soverane sueit thing, quhy sleip ȝe no betir?
Me think ther haldis ȝow a hete, as ȝe sum harme alyt.'
Quoth I, 'My hony, hald abak, and handill me nought sair;
A hache is happinit hastely at my hert rut.'
With that I seme for to swoune, thought I na swerf tak;   225
And thus beswik I that swane with my sueit wordis:
I cast on him a crabit E, quhen cleir day is cummyn,
And lettis it is a luf blenk, quhen he about glemys,
I turne it in a tender luke, that I in tene warit,
And him behaldis hamely with hertly smyling.   230
I wald a tender peronall, that myght na put thole,
That hatit men with hard geir for hurting of flesch,
Had my gud man to hir gest; for I dar God suer,
Scho suld not stert for his straik a stray breid of erd.
And syne, I wald that ilk band, that ȝe so blist call,   235
Had bund him so to that bryght, quhill his bak werkit;
And I wer in a beid broght with berne that me likit,
I trow that bird of my blis suld a bourd want.
  Onone, quhen this amyable had endit hir speche,
Ludly lauchand the laif allowit hir mekle: 240

---

206 *vacandis*, open to new tenants   213 *walteris*, toss   214 *wariand*, cursing
215 *craudoune*, coward   216 *kenrik*, kingdom   219 *tume*, empty   220 *ȝoldin*
ȝerd, empty penis   222 *ther haldis ȝow a hete*, you have a fever; *alyt*, suffered
224 *hache*, ache   225 *swerf*, faint   226 *beswik*, deceive   228 *lettis*, pretend
229 *tene*, vexation   230 *hamely*, kindly   231 *peronall*, young whore
234 *straik*, thrust   236 *werkit*, heaved   237 *beid*, bed   240 *laif*, others

Thir gay wiffis maid game amang the grene leiffis;
Thai drank and did away dule under derne bewis;
Thai swapit of the sueit wyne, thai swanquhit of hewis,
Bot all the pertlyar in plane thai put out ther vocis.
Than said the Weido, I wis ther is no way othir;   245
Now tydis me for to talk; my taill it is nixt:
God my spreit now inspir and my speche quykkin,
And send me sentence to say substantious and noble;
Sa that my preching may pers 30ur perverst hertis,
And mak 30u mekar to men in maneris and conditiounis.   250
   I schaw 30w, sisteris in schrift, I wes a schrew evir,
Bot I wes schene in my schrowd, and schew me innocent;
And thought I dour wes, and dane, dispitois, and bald,
I wes dissymblit suttelly in a sanctis liknes:
I semyt sober, and sueit, and sempill without fraud,   255
Bot I couth sexty dissaif that suttillar wer haldin.
   Unto my lesson 3e lyth, and leir at me wit,
Gif you nought list be forleit with losingeris untrew:
Be constant in 30ur governance, and counterfeit gud maneris,
Thought 3e be kene, inconstant, and cruell of mynd;   260
Thought 3e as tygris be terne, be tretable in luf,
And be as turtoris in your talk, thought 3e haif talis brukill;
Be dragonis baith and dowis ay in double forme,
And quhen it nedis 30w, onone, note baith ther stranthis;
Be amyable with humble face, as angellis apperand,   265
And with a terrebill tail be stangand as edderis;
Be of 30ur luke like innocentis, thoght 3e haif evill myndis;
Be courtly ay in clething and costly arrayit,
That hurtis 30w nought worth a hen; 30wr husband pays for all.
   Twa husbandis haif I had, thai held me baith deir,   270
Thought I dispytit thaim agane, thai spyit it na thing:
Ane wes ane hair hogeart, that hostit out flewme;
I hatit him like a hund, thought I it hid preve:
With kissing and with clapping I gert the carll fone;

242 *dule*, grief   243 *swapit*, drank; *swanquhit*, swanwhite   253 *dane*, reserved;
dispitois, cruel   256 *suttillar*, cleverer   257 *lyth*, listen   258 *forleit*,
abandoned; *losingeris*, deceivers   260 *kene*, savage   261 *terne*, fierce   262
turtoris, turtle-doves; *talis brukill*, yielding tails   263 *dowis*, doves   264
stranthis, virtues   272 *hair hogeart*, hoary, knackered old man; *hostit*, coughed
273 *preve*, secretly   274 *carll fone*, fellow play the fool

Weil couth I krych his cruke bak, and kemm his kewt noddill,
And with a bukky in my cheik bo on him behind,   276
And with a bek gang about and bler his ald E,
And with a kyind contynance kys his crynd chekis;
In to my mynd makand mokis at that mad fader,
Trouand me with trew lufe to treit him so fair.   280
This cought I do without dule and na dises tak,
Bot ay be mery in my mynd and myrthfull of cher.
   I had a lufsummar leid my lust for to slokyn,
That couth be secrete and sure and ay saif my honour,
And sew bot at certayne tymes and in sicir placis;   285
Ay when the ald did me anger, with akword wordis,
Apon the galland for to goif it gladit me agane.
I had sic wit that for wo weipit I litill,
Bot leit the sueit ay the sour to gud sesone bring.
Quhen that the chuf wald me chid, with girnand chaftis,   290
I wald him chuk, cheik and chyn, and cheris him so mekill,
That his cheif chymys he had chevist to my sone,
Suppos the churll wes gane chaist, or the child wes gottin:
As wis woman ay I wrought and not as wod fule,
For mar with wylis I wan na wichtnes of handis.   295
   Syne maryit I a marchand, myghti of gudis:
He was a man of myd eld, and of mene statur;
Bot we na fallowis wer in frendschip or blud,
In fredome, na furth bering, na fairnes of persoune,
Quhilk ay the fule did forʒet, for febilnes of knawlege,   300
Bot I sa oft thoght him on, quhill angrit his hert,
And quhilum I put furth my voce and Pedder him callit:
I wald ryght tuichandly talk be I wes tuyse maryit,
For endit wes my innocence with my ald husband:
I wes apperand to be pert within perfit eild;   305
Sa sais the curat of our kirk, that knew me full ʒing:
He is our famous to be fals, that fair worthy prelot;
I salbe laith to lat him le, quhill I may luke furth.

---

275 *krych*, scratch; *kewt*, cropped   276 *bukky ... cheik*, tongue in cheek; *bo on*,
make a face at   277 *bek*, curtsy   278 *crynd*, shrunken   280 *trouand*, thinking
281 *cought*, could; *dule*, trouble; *dises*, hardship   283 *lufsummar leid*, more
lovable man   285 *sew*, attend; *sicir*, safe   287 *goif*, gaze   290 *chuf*, churl
292 *chymys*, manor; *chevist*, transfer to   293 *suppos*, although   295 *mar*, more;
wichtnes, strength   299 *furth bering*, conduct   303 *tuichandly*, touchingly
305 *within perfit eild*, before I was of full age

I gert the buthman obey, ther wes no bute ellis;
He maid me ryght hie reverens, fra he my rycht knew: 310
For, thocht I say it my self, the severance wes mekle
Betuix his bastard blude and my birth noble.
That page wes nevir of sic price for to presome anys
Unto my persone to be peir, had pete nought grantit.
Bot mercy in to womanheid is a mekle vertu,   315
For never bot in a gentill hert is generit ony ruth.
I held ay grene in to his mynd that I of grace tuk him,
And for he couth ken him self I curtasly him lerit:
He durst not sit anys my summondis, for, or the secund charge,
He wes ay redy for to ryn, so rad he wes for blame.   320
Bot ay my will wes the war of womanly natur;
The mair he loutit for my luf, the les of him I rakit;
And eik, this is a ferly thing, or I him faith gaif,
I had sic favour to that freke, and feid syne for ever.

Quhen I the cure had all clene and him ourcummyn haill, 325
I crew abone that craudone, as cok that wer victour;
Quhen I him saw subject and sett at myn bydding,
Than I him lichtlyit as a lowne and lathit his maneris.
Than woxe I sa unmerciable to martir him I thought,
For as a best I broddit him to all boyis laubour;   330
I wald haif ridden him to Rome with raip in his heid,
Wer not ruffill of my renoune and rumour of pepill.
And 3it hatrent I hid within my hert all;
Bot quhilis it hepit so huge, quhill it behud out:
3it tuk I nevir the wosp clene out of my wyde throte,   335
Quhill I oucht wantit of my will or quhat I wald desir.
Bot quhen I severit had that syre of substance in erd,
And gottin his biggingis to my barne, and hie burrow landis,
Than with a stew stert out the stoppell of my hals,
That he all stunyst throu the stound, as of a stele wappin.   340
Than wald I, efter lang, first sa fane haif bene wrokin,
That I to flyte wes als fers as a fell dragoun.
I had for flattering of that fule fen3eit so lang,

---

309 *buthman*, shopkeeper   314 *pete*, pity   320 *rad*, afraid   321 *war*, worse
322 *loutit*, humbled himself; *rakit*, thought   323 *ferly*, strange   324 *feid*, hostility
325 *cure*, task   328 *lichtlyit*, despised; *lowne*, wretch   330 *best*, beast; *broddit*,
goaded   332 *ruffill*, destruction   334 *behud*, burst   335 *wosp*, wisp of straw
used as stopper   338 *biggingis*, buildings   339 *stew*, ?stink; *stert out*, out
started; *hals*, throat   340 *stunyst*, was astonished   341 *wrokin*, revenged

Mi evidentis of heritagis or thai wer all selit,
My breist, that wes gret beild, bowdyn wes sa huge,   345
That neir my baret out brist or the band makin.
Bot quhen my billis and my bauchlis wes all braid selit,
I wald na langar beir on bridill, bot braid up my heid;
Thar myght na molet mak me moy, na hald my mouth in:
I gert the ren3eis rak and rif into sondir;   350
I maid that wif carll to werk all womenis werkis,
And laid all manly materis and mensk in this eird.
Than said I to my cummaris in counsall about, ·
'Se how I cabeld 3one cout with a kene brydill!
The cappill, that the crelis kest in the caf mydding,   355
Sa curtasly the cart drawis, and kennis na plungeing,
He is nought skeich, na 3it sker, na scippis nought one syd':
And thus the scorne and the scaith scapit he nothir.
    He wes no glaidsum gest for a gay lady,
Tharfor I gat him a game that ganyt him bettir;   360
He wes a gret goldit man and of gudis riche;
I leit him be my lumbart to lous me all misteris,
And he wes fane for to fang fra me that fair office,
And thoght my favoris to fynd through his feill giftis.
He grathit me in a gay silk and gudly arrayis,   365
In gownis of engranyt clayth and gret goldin chen3eis,
In ringis ryally set with riche ruby stonis,
Quhill hely raise my renoune amang the rude peple.
Bot I full craftely did keip thai courtly wedis,
Quhill efter dede of that drowp, that dotht nought in chalmir:
Thought he of all my clathis maid cost and expense,   371
Ane othir sall the worschip haif, that weildis me eftir;
And thoght I likit him bot litill, 3it for luf of otheris,
I wald me prun a plesandly in precius wedis,
That luffaris myght apone me luke and 3ing lusty gallandis, 375
That I held more in daynte and derer be ful mekill

___

344 *mi evidentis ... selit,* till the deeds of the inheritance were all sealed   345
beild, bowdyn, swollen   346 *baret,* anger; *band,* bond   347 *bauchlis,*
?documents   349 *molet,* curb; *moy,* meek   350 *rak,* stretch; *rif,* tear   352
mensk, dignity; *eird,* earth   354 *cabeld,* secured; *cout,* colt   355 *cappill,* horse;
crelis kest, overthrew the wickerwork panniers; *caf mydding,* chaff midden   357
skeich, spirited; *sker,* restive; *scippis,* skips   360 *ganyt,* suited   361 *goldit,*
wealthy   362 *lumbart,* financier   364 *feill,* many   370 *drowp,* feeble fellow
374 *prun3a,* preen

Ne him that dressit me so dink: full dotit wes his heyd.
Quhen he wes heryit out of hand to hie up my honoris,
And payntit me as pako, proudest of fedderis,
I him miskennyt, be Crist, and cukkald him maid;   380
I him forleit as a lad and lathlyit him mekle:
I thoght my self a papingay and him a plukit herle;
All thus enforsit he his fa and fortifyit in strenth,
And maid a stalwart staff to strik him selfe doune.

   Bot of ane bowrd in to bed I sall ʒow breif ʒit: 385
Quhen he ane hal ʒear was hanyt, and him behuffit rage,
And I wes laith to be loppin with sic a lob avoir,
Alse lang as he wes one loft, I lukit on him nevir,
Na leit never enter in my thoght that he my thing persit,
Bot ay in mynd ane other man ymagynit that I haid;   390
Or ellis had I never mery bene at that myrthles raid.
Quhen I that grome geldit had of gudis and of natur,
Me thought him gracelese one to goif, sa me God help:
Quhen he had warit all one me his welth and his substance,
Me thoght his wit wes all went away with the laif;   395
And so I did him dispise, I spittit quhen I saw
That super spendit evill spreit, spulʒeit of all vertu.
For, weill ʒe wait, wiffis, that he that wantis riches
And valʒeandnes in Venus play, is ful vile haldin:
Full fruster is his fresch array and fairnes of persoune,   400
All is bot frutlese his effeir and falʒeis at the up with.
I buskit up my barnis like baronis sonnis,
And maid bot fulis of the fry of his first wif.
I banyst fra my boundis his brethir ilkane;
His frendis as my fais I held at feid evir;   405
Be this, ʒe beleif may, I luffit nought him self,
For nevir I likit a leid that langit till his blude:
And ʒit thir wismen, thai wait that all wiffis evill
Ar kend with ther conditionis and knawin with the samin.

377 *dink*, daintily   378 *heryit*, plundered   379 *pako*, peacock   380 *miskennyt*,
neglected   381 *forleit*, abandoned; *lad*, menial   382 *papingay*, parrot; *plukit*
herle, plucked heron   383 *enforsit*, gave power to; *fa*, enemy   385 *bowrd*, jest;
breif, tell   386 *hanyt*, held back   387 *loppin*, mounted; *lob avoir*, clumsy
carthorse   388 *one loft*, on top of me   389 *thing*, genitals   392 *grome*, fellow
393 *goif*, gaze at   397 *super spendit*, spent more than he had; *spulʒeit*, despoiled
400 *fruster*, useless   401 *up with*, climax   403 *fry*, children   408/9 *thai*
wait...samin, they know that all bad wives are proclaimed by their habits and
known by them

Deid is now that dyvour and dollin in erd: 410
With him deit all my dule and my drery thoghtis;
Now done is my dolly nyght, my day is upsprungin,
Adew dolour, adew! my daynte now begynis:
Now am I a wedow, I wise and weill am at ese;
I weip as I were woful, but wel is me for ever;   415
I busk as I wer bailfull, bot blith is my hert;
My mouth it makis murnyng, and my mynd lauchis;
My clokis thai ar caerfull in colour of sabill,
Bot courtly and ryght curyus my corse is ther undir:
I drup with a ded luke in my dule habit,   420
As with manis daill [I] had done for dayis of my lif.
   Quhen that I go to the kirk, cled in cair weid,
As foxe in a lambis fleise fenȝe I my cheir;
Than lay I furght my bright buke one breid one my kne,
With mony lusty letter ellummynit with gold;   425
And drawis my clok forthwart our my face quhit,
That I may spy, unaspyit, a space me beside:
Full oft I blenk by my buke, and blynis of devotioun,
To se quhat berne is best brand or bredest in schulderis,
Or forgeit is maist forcely to furnyse a bancat   430
In Venus chalmer, valȝeandly, withoutin vane ruse:
And, as the new mone all pale, opressit with change,
Kythis quhilis her cleir face through cluddis of sable,
So keik I through my clokis, and castis kynd lukis
To knychtis, and to cleirkis, and cortly personis.   435
   Quhen frendis of my husbandis behaldis me one fer,
I haif a wattir spunge for wa, within my wyde clokis,
Than wring I it full wylely and wetis my chekis,
With that watteris myn ene and welteris doune teris.
Than say thai all that sittis about, 'Se ȝe nought, allace! 440
ȝone lustlese led: so lelely scho luffit hir husband:
ȝone is a pete to enprent in a princis hert,
That sic a perle of plesance suld ȝone pane dre!'
I sane me as I war any sanct, and semys ane angell;

---

410 *dyvour*, bankrupt; *dollin*, buried   412 *dolly*, dreary   416 *busk*, dress;
bailfull, sorrowful   420 *drup*, droop   421 *daill*, intercourse   422 *cair*,
mourning   424 *one breid*, open   428 *blynis of*, cease from   429 *brand*,
muscled   433 *kythis*, shows   436 *one fer*, afar   441 *lustlese led*, joyless
woman   442 *pete*, cause for pity   444 *sane me*, cross myself

At langage of lichory I leit as I war crabit: 445
I sich, without sair hert or seiknes in body;
According to my sable weid I mon haif sad maneris,
Or thai will se all the suth; for certis, we wemen
We set us all fra the syght to syle men of treuth:
We dule for na evill deid, sa it be derne haldin.   450
  Wise wemen has wayis and wonderfull gydingis
With gret engyne to bejaip ther jolyus husbandis;
And quyetly, with sic craft, convoyis our materis
That, under Crist, no creatur kennis of our doingis.
Bot folk a cury may miscuke, that knawlege wantis,   455
And has na colouris for to cover thair awne kindly fautis;
As dois thir damysellis, for derne dotit lufe,
That dogonis haldis in dainte and delis with thaim so lang,
Quhill all the cuntre knaw ther kyndnes and faith:
Faith has a fair name, bot falsheid faris bettir: 460
Fy one hir that can nought feyne her fame for to saif!
3it am I wise in sic werk and wes all my tyme;
Thoght I want wit in warldlynes, I wylis haif in luf,
As ony happy woman has that is of hie blude:
Hutit be the halok lase a hunder 3eir of eild!   465
  I have ane secrete servand, rycht sobir of his toung,
That me supportis of sic nedis, quhen I a syne mak:
Thoght he be sympill to the sicht, he has a tong sickir;
Full mony semelyar sege wer service dois mak:
Thought I haif cair, undir cloke, the cleir day quhill nyght, 470
3it haif I solace, undir serk, quhill the sone ryse.
3it am I haldin a haly wif our all the haill schyre,
I am sa peteouse to the pur, quhen ther is personis mony.
In passing of pilgrymage I pride me full mekle,
Mair for the prese of peple na ony perdoun wynyng.   475
   Bot 3it me think the best bourd, quhen baronis and knychtis,
And othir bachilleris blith blumyng in 3outh,
And all my luffaris lele, my lugeing persewis,
And fyllis me wyne wantonly with weilfair and joy: ·

---

445 *lichory*, lechery; *leit*, behave; *crabit*, angry   449 *syle*, blind   450 *dule*,
mourn; *derne*, secret   452 *bejaip*, fool; *jolyus*, jealous   455 *cury*, cooked dish
456 *kindly*, natural   457 *dotit*, stupid   458 *dogonis*, worthless men; *delis*, have
to do with   463 *warldlynes*, worldly matters   465 *hutit*, despised; *halok*,
guileless   468 *sympill*, guileless   469 *sege*, man; *wer*, worse   476 *bourd*, jest
478 *lugeing*, lodging; *persewis*, come to

Sum rownis, and sum ralʒeis and sum redis ballatis;   480
Sum raiffis furght rudly with riatus speche;
Sum plenis, and sum prayis; sum prasis mi bewte,
Sum kissis me; sum clappis me; sum kyndnes me proferis;
Sum kerffis to me curtasli; sum me the cop giffis;
Sum stalwardly steppis ben, with a stout curage,   485
And a stif standand thing staiffis in my neiff;
And mony blenkis ben our, that but full fer sittis,
That mai, for the thik thrang, nought thrif as thai wald.
Bot, with my fair calling, I comfort thaim all:
For he that sittis me nixt, I nip on his finger;   490
I serf him on the tothir syde on the samin fasson;
And he that behind me sittis, I hard on him lene;
And him befor with my fut fast on his I stramp
And to the bernis far but sueit blenkis I cast:
To every man in speciall speke I sum wordis   495
So wisly and womanly, quhill warmys ther hertis.
Thar is no liffand leid so law of degre
That sall me luf unluffit, I am so luik hertit;
And gif his lust so be lent into my lyre quhit,
That he be lost or with me lig, his lif sall not danger.   500
I am so mercifull in mynd, and menys all wichtis,
My sely saull salbe saif, quhen Sabot all jugis.
Ladyis leir thir lessonis and be no lassis fundin:
This is the legeand of my lif, thought Latyne it be nane.
    Quhen endit had her ornat speche, this eloquent wedow, 505
Lowd thai lewch all the laif, and loffit hir mekle;
And said thai sald exampill tak of her soverane teching,
And wirk efter hir wordis, that woman wes so prudent.
Than culit thai ther mouthis with confortable drinkis;
And carpit full cummerlik with cop going round.   510
    Thus draif thai our that deir nyght with danceis full noble,
Quhill that the day did up daw, and dew donkit flouris;
The morow myld wes and meik, the mavis did sing,
And all remuffit the myst, and the meid smellit;

---

480 *rownis*, whispers; *ralʒeis*, jests   481 *raiffis*, rant   482 *plenis*, complain
484 *kerffis*, carve   486 *staiffis*, thrusts; *neiff*, fist   487 *blenkis*, glance; *ben our*,
over to the inner room; *full fer*, too far away   494 *far but*, further out
498 *luik*, warm   499 *lyre*, skin   501 *menys*, pity   502 *Sabot*, God
510 *carpit*, chatted   511 *draif*, spent   512 *donkit*, dampened

Silver schouris doune schuke as the schene cristall,   515
And berdis schoutit in schaw with thair schill notis;
The goldin glitterand gleme so gladit ther hertis,
Thai maid a glorius gle amang the grene bewis.
The soft sowch of the swyr and soune of the stremys,
The sueit savour of the sward singing of foulis,   520
Myght confort ony creatur of the kyn of Adam,
And kindill agane his curage, thocht it wer cald sloknyt.
Than rais thir ryall rosis, in ther riche wedis,
And rakit hame to ther rest through the rise blumys;
And I all prevely past to a plesand arber,   525
And with my pen did report thair pastance most mery.

ȝe auditoris most honorable, that eris has gevin
Oneto this uncouth aventur, quhilk airly me happinnit;
Of thir thre wantoun wiffis, that I haif writtin heir,
Quhilk wald ȝe waill to ȝour wif, gif ȝe suld wed one?   530

518 *bewis*, boughs   519 *sowch*, murmur of breeze; *swyr*, glen   522 *sloknyt*, quenched   524 *rakit*, went; *rise blumys*, flowering twigs   528 *uncouth*, strange   530 *waill*, choose

83

28. QUHAT IS THIS LYFE

Quhat is this lyfe bot ane straucht way to deid,
Quhilk hes a tyme to pas, and nane to duell;
A slyding quheill us lent to seik remeid;
A fre chois gevin to Paradice or Hell;
A pray to deid, quhome vane is to repell;   5
A schoirt torment for infineit glaidnes,
Als schort ane joy for lestand hevynes.

1 *straucht*, straight   5 *pray*, prey   7 *lestand*, lasting

29. SWEIT ROIS OF VERTEW

Sweit rois of vertew and of gentilnes,
Delytsum lyllie of everie lustynes
Richest in bontie and in bewtie cleir
And everie vertew that is deir
Except onlie that 3e are mercyles   5

In to 3our garthe this day I did persew
Thair saw I flowris that fresche wer of hew
Baithe quhyte and rid moist lusty wer to seyne
And halsum herbis upone stalkis grene
3it leif nor flour fynd could I nane of rew.   10

I dout that merche with his caild blastis keyne
Hes slane this gentill herbe that I of mene
Quhois petewous deithe dois to my hart sic pane
That I wald mak to plant his rute agane
So confortand his levis unto me bene.   15

3 *bontie*, goodness   6 *garthe*, garden; *persew*, come   10 *rew*, rue

30. INCONSTANCY OF LUVE

Quha will behald of luve the chance
With sueit dissavyng countenance
In quhais fair dissimulance
    May none assure;
Quhilk is begun with inconstance   5
And endis nocht but variance;
Scho haldis with continuance
    No serviture.

Discretioun and considerance
Ar both out of hir govirnance,   10
Quhairfoir of it the schort plesance
    May nocht indure;
Scho is so new of acquentance,
The auld gais fra remembrance;
Thus I gife our the observans   15
    Of luvis cure.

It is ane pount of ignorance
To lufe in sic distemperance,
Sen tyme mispendit may avance
    No creature;   20
In luve to keip allegance,
It war als nys an ordinance,
As quha wald bid ane deid man dance
    In sepulture.

6 *variance*, discord   16 *cure*, office, task   17 *pount*, sign

The Dance of the Sevin Deidly Synnis

Off Februar the fyiftene nycht,
Full lang befoir the dayis lycht,
    I lay in till a trance;
And then I saw baith hevin and hell:
Me thocht, amangis the feyndis fell,   5
    Mahoun gart cry ane dance
Off schrewis that wer nevir schrevin,
Aganis the feist of Fasternis evin
    To mak thair observance;
He bad gallandis ga graith a gyis,   10
And kast up gamountis in the skyis,
    That last came out of France.

'Lat se,' quod he, 'Now quha begynnis';
With that the fowll Sevin Deidly Synnis
    Begowth to leip at anis.   15
And first of all in dance wes **Pryd**,
With hair wyld bak and bonet on syd,
    Lyk to mak waistie wanis;
And round abowt him, as a quheill,
Hang all in rumpillis to the heill   20
    His kethat for the nanis:
Mony prowd trumpour with him trippit,
Throw skaldand fyre ay as thay skippit
    Thay gyrnd with hiddous granis.

Heilie harlottis on hawtane wyis   25
Come in with mony sindrie gyis,
    Bot ȝit luche nevir Mahoun,
Quhill preistis come in with bair schevin nekkis,
Than all the feyndis lewche and maid gekkis,
    Blak Belly and Bawsy Broun.   30

---

7 *schrewis*, evildoers; *schrevin*, shriven   10 *graith a gyis*, prepare a masquerade
11 *gamountis*, capers   18 *waistie wanis*, ruined homes   20 *rumpillis*, folds
21 *kethat*, cloak   22 *trumpour*, deceiver   24 *granis*, groans   25 *heilie*, proud;
hawtane, haughty   27 *luche*, laughed   29 *gekkis*, gestures

Than **Yre** come in with sturt and stryfe;
His hand wes ay upoun his knyfe,
    He brandeist lyk a beir:
Bostaris, braggaris, and barganeris,
Eftir him passit in to pairis,   35
    All bodin in feir of weir;
In jakkis, and scryppis and bonettis of steill,
Thair leggis wer chenȝeit to the heill,
    Frawart wes thair affeir:
Sum upoun udir with brandis beft,   ·   40
Sum jaggit uthiris to the heft,
    With knyvis that scherp cowd scheir.

Nixt in the dance followit **Invy**,
Fild full of feid and fellony,
    Hid malyce and dispyte;   45
For pryvie hatrent that tratour trymlit.
Him followit mony freik dissymlit,
    With fenȝeit wirdis quhyte;
And flatteris in to menis facis;
And bakbyttaris in secreit places,   50
    To ley that had delyte;
And rownaris of fals lesingis;
Allace! that courtis of noble kingis
    Of thame can nevir be quyte.

31 *Yre*, Ire; *sturt*, violence   34 *bostaris*, boasters   36 *bodin*, armed; *in feir of*
weir, in a warlike way   39 *frawart*, froward; *affeir*, manner   40 *beft*, struck
41 *heft*, handle, hilt   44 *feid*, hostility   47 *freik*, man; *dissymlit*, disguised
48 *fenȝeit wirdis quhyte*, feigned insincere words   51 *ley*, lie   52 *rownaris*,
whisperers; *lesingis*, lies   54 *quyte*, quit

Nixt him in dans come **Cuvatyce**, 55
Rute of all evill and grund of vyce,
   That nevir cowd be content;
Catyvis, wrechis, and ockeraris,
Hud-pykis, hurdaris, and gadderaris,
   All with that warlo went: 60
Out of thair throttis thay schot on udder
Hett moltin gold, me thocht a fudder,
   As fyreflawcht maist fervent;
Ay as they tomit thame of schot,
Feyndis fild thame new up to the thrott 65
   With gold of allkin prent.

Syne **Sweirnes**, at the secound bidding,
Come lyk a sow out of a midding,
   Full slepy wes his grunȝie:
Mony sweir bumbard belly huddroun, 70
Mony slute daw and slepy duddroun,
   Him servit ay with sounȝie;
He drew thame furth in till a chenȝie,
And Belliall, with a brydill renȝie,
   Evir lascht thame on the lunȝie: 75
In dance thay war so slaw of feit,
Thay gaif thame in the fyre a heit,
   And maid thame quicker of counȝie.

---

55 *Cuvatyce, Covetise,* Greed   58 *ockeraris,* usurers   59 *hud-pykis,* misers;
hurdaris, hoarders of money   60 *warlo,* warlock   61 *on udder,* on each other
62 *fudder,* cartload   63 *fyreflawcht,* lightning   64 *tomit,* emptied; *schot,*
discharge   66 *prent,* stamp   67 *Sweirnes,* Sloth   69 *grunȝie,* snout
70 *bumbard,* idle; *belly huddroun,* big-bellied glutton   71 *slute daw,* dirty slut;
duddroun, sloven   72 *sounȝie,* delay   73 *chenȝie,* chain   74 *renȝie,* rein
75 *lunȝie,* loins   78 *counȝie,* movement

Than **Lichery**, that lathly cors,
Come berand lyk a bagit hors,
    And Ydilnes did him leid;   80
Thair wes with him ane ugly sort,
And mony stynkand fowll tramort,
    That had in syn bene deid.
Quhen thay wer entrit in the dance,   85
Thay wer full strenge of countenance,
    Lyk turkas birnand reid;
All led thay uthir by the tersis,
Suppois thay fycket with thair ersis,
    It mycht be na remeid.   90

Than the fowll monstir **Glutteny**,
Off wame unsasiable and gredy,
    To dance he did him dres:
Him followit mony fowll drunckart,
With can and collep, cop and quart,   95
    In surffet and exces;
Full mony a waistles wallydrag,
With wamis unweildable, did furth wag,
    In creische that did incres;
'Drynk!' ay thay cryit, with mony a gaip,   100
The feyndis gaif thame hait leid to laip,
    Thair lovery wes na les.

Na menstrallis playit to thame but dowt,
For glemen thair wer haldin owt,
    Be day and eik by nycht;   105
Except a menstrall that slew a man,
Swa till his heretage he wan,
    And entirt be breif of richt.

---

80 *berand*, crying; *bagit hors*, stallion   83 *tramort*, decomposing corpse
87 *turkas*, smith's pincers   88 *tersis*, penises   89 *fycket*, fucked   92 *wame*,
belly; *unsasiable*, insatiable   95 *collep*, slice of meat   97 *waistles wallydrag*,
obese sloven   99 *creische*, grease   102 *lovery*, bounty

Than cryd Mahoun for a Heleand padȝane;
Syne ran a feynd to feche Makfadȝane,   110
    Far northwart in a nuke;
Be he the correnoch had done schout,
Erschemen so gadderit him abowt,
    In Hell grit rowme thay tuke.
Thae tarmegantis with tag and tatter   115
Full lowd in Ersche begowth to clatter,
    And rowp lyk revin and ruke:
The Devill sa devit wes with thair ȝell,
That in the depest pot of hell
    He smorit thame with smuke.   120

The Sowtar and Tailȝouris War

Nixt that a turnament wes tryid,
That lang befoir in hell wes cryid,
    In presens of Mahoun;
Betuix a telȝour and ane sowtar,
A pricklous and ane hobbell clowttar,   125
    The barres wes maid boun.
The tailȝeour, baith with speir and scheild,
Convoyit wes unto the feild
    With mony lymmar loun,
Off seme byttaris and beist knapparis,   130
Off stomok steillaris and clayth takkaris,
    A graceles garisoun.

109 *padȝane*, pageant   112 *correnoch*, lament, loud outcry   113 *Erschemen*,
Highlanders   115 *tag and tatter*, rags and tatters   116 *Ersche*, Gaelic
117 *rowp*, croak; *revin*, raven   118 *devit*, deafened   120 *smorit*, smothered
124 *telȝour*, tailor; *sowtar*, cobbler   125 *hobbell clowttar*, shoe-patcher
126 *barres*, lists; *boun*, ready   129 *lymmar loun*, scoundrelly rogue   130 *seme
byttaris*, seam-biters; *beist knapparis*, basting stitchers   131 *steillaris*, workers

His baner born wes him befoir,
Quhairin wes clowttis ane hundreth scoir,
   Ilk ane of divers hew;   135
And all stowin out of sindry webbis,
For, quhill the greik sie flowis and ebbis,
   Telȝouris will nevir be trew.
The tailȝour on the barrowis blent,
Allais! he tynt all hardyment,   140
   For feir he chaingit hew:
Mahoun come furth and maid him knycht,
Na ferly thocht his hart wes licht,
   That to sic honor grew.

The tailȝeour hecht befoir Mahoun   145
That he suld ding the sowtar doun,
   Thocht he wer strang as mast;
Bot quhen he on the barrowis blenkit,
The telȝoris curage a littill schrenkit,
   His hairt did all ourcast.   150
Quhen to the sowtar he did cum,
Off all sic wirdis he wes full dum,
   So soir he wes agast;
In harte he tuke ȝit sic ane scunner,
Ane rak of fartis, lyk ony thunner,   155
   Went fra him, blast for blast.

134 *clowttis*, rags   136 *stowin*, stolen   139 *barrowis*, lists; *blent*, blinked
140 *hardyment*, courage   143 *ferly*, wonder   145 *hecht*, swore   154 *scunner*,
loathing   155 *rak*, volley

The sowtar to the feild him drest,
He wes convoyid out of the west,
    As ane defender stout:
Suppois he had na lusty varlot,   160
He had full mony lowsy harlott
    Round rynnand him aboute.
His banner wes of barkit hyd,
Quhairin Sanct Girnega did glyd
    Befoir that rebald rowt: 165
Full sowttarlyk he wes of laitis,
For ay betuix the harnes plaitis
    The uly birstit out.

Quhen on the telȝour he did luke,
His hairt a littill dwamyng tuke,   170
    He mycht nocht rycht upsitt;
In to his stommok wes sic ane steir,
Off all his dennar, quhilk he coft deir,
    His breist held deill a bitt.
To comfort him, or he raid forder,   175
The Devill off knychtheid gaif him order,
    For sair syne he did spitt,
And he about the devillis nek
Did spew agane ane quart of blek,
    Thus knychtly he him quitt.   180

Than fourty tymis the Feynd cryd, Fy!
The sowtar rycht effeiritly
    Unto the feild he socht:
Quhen thay wer servit of thair speiris,
Folk had ane feill be thair effeiris,   185
    Thair hairtis wer baith on flocht.
Thay spurrit thair hors on adir syd,
Syne thay attour the grund cowd glyd,
    Than thame togidder brocht;
The tailȝeour that wes nocht weill sittin,   190
He left his sadill all beschittin,
    And to the grund he socht.

160 *varlot*, squire   161 *harlott*, rascal   163 *barkit*, hardened   164 *Girnega*, a
devil   166 *laitis*, manner   168 *uly*, oil   170 *dwamyng*, faintness   173 *coft*,
bought   179 *blek*, blacking   182 *effeiritly*, in alarm   185 *feill*, suspicion;
effeiris, behaviour   186 *on flocht*, in a flutter

His harnas brak and maid ane brattill,
The sowtaris hors scart with the rattill,
    And round about cowd reill;   195
The beist that frayit wes rycht evill,
Ran with the sowtar to the Devill,
    And he rewardit him weill.
Sum thing frome him the Feynd eschewit,
He went agane to bene bespewit,   200
    So stern he wes in steill:
He thocht he wald agane debait him,
He turnd his ers and all bedret him,
    Evin quyte from nek till heill.

He lowsit it of with sic a reird,   205
Baith hors and man he straik till eird,
    He fartit with sic ane feir;
'Now haif I quitt the,' quod Mahoun;
Thir new maid knychtis lay bayth in swoun,
    And did all armes mensweir.   210
The Devill gart thame to dungeoun dryve,
And thame of knychtheid cold depryve,
    Dischairgeing thame of weir;
And maid thame harlottis bayth for evir,
Quhilk still to keip thay had fer levir,   215
    Nor ony armes beir.

I had mair of thair werkis writtin,
Had nocht the sowtar bene beschittin
    With Belliallis ers unblist;
Bot that sa gud ane bourd me thocht,   220
Sic solace to my hairt it rocht,
    For lawchtir neir I brist;
Quhairthrow I walknit of my trance
To put this in rememerance,
    Mycht no man me resist,   225
For this said justing it befell
Befoir Mahoun, the air of hell:
    Now trow this gif ʒe list.

193 *brattill*, clatter   196 *frayit*, scared   199 *eschewit*, avoided   203 *bedret*,
shitted on   205 *reird*, news   207 *feir*, violence   210 *mensweir*, renounce
215 *still*, style   227 *air*, heir

The Amendis to the Tailʒouris and Sowtaris
for the turnament maid on thame

Betuix twell houris and ellevin
I dremed ane angell came fra hevin   230
With plesand stevin sayand on hie,
    'Telʒouris and sowtaris blist be ʒe.

In hevin hie ordand is ʒour place
Aboif all sanctis in grit solace,   235
Nixt God grittest in dignitie;
    Tailʒouris and sowtaris blist be ʒe.

The caus to ʒow is nocht unkend:
That God mismakkis ʒe do amend
Be craft and grit agilitie;   240
    Tailʒouris and sowtaris blist be ʒe.

Sowtaris, with schone weill maid and meit
ʒe mend the faltis of illmaid feit;
Quhairfoir to hevin ʒour saulis will fle;
    Telʒouris and sowtaris blist be ʒe.   245

Is nocht in all this fair a flyrok
That hes upoun his feit a wyrok,
Knowll tais nor mowlis in no degrie
    Bot ye can hyd thame, blist be ʒe.

And ʒe, tailʒouris, with weillmaid clais   250
Can mend the werst maid man that gais
And mak him semely for to se,
    Telʒouris and sowtaris blist be ʒe.

Thocht God mak ane misfassonit man,
ʒe can him all schaip new agane   255
And fassoun him betir be sic thre,
    Telʒouris and sowtaris blist be ʒe.

231 *stevin*, voice   234 *ordand*, ordained   239 *That*, what   246 *flyrok*,
deformed person   247 *wyrok*, corn   248 *knowll tais*, swollen toes; *mowlis*,
chilblains

Thocht a man haif a brokin bak,
Haif he a gude crafty tel3our, quhattrak,
That can it cuver with craftis slie;   260
    Tel3ouris and sowtaris, blist be 3e.

Off God grit kyndness may 3e clame
That helpis his peple fra cruke and lame,
Supportand faltis with 3our supple,
    Tail3ouris and sowtaris, blist be 3e.   265

In erd 3e kyth sic mirakillis heir
In hevin 3e salbe sanctis cleir,
Thocht 3e be knavis in this cuntre,
    Tel3ouris and sowtaris blist be 3ie.'

Off Lentren in the first mornyng,
Airly as did the day up spring,
Thus sang ane bird with voce out plane,
   'All erdly joy returnis in pane.

'O man, haif mynd that thow mon pas;   5
Remembir that thow art bot ass,
And sall in ass return agane,
   All erdly joy returnis in pane.

'Haif mynd that eild ay followis ȝowth;
Deth followis lyfe with gaipand mowth,   10
Devoring fruct and flowring grane;
   All erdly joy returnis in pane.

'Welth, warldly gloir, and riche array
Ar all bot thornis laid in thy way,
Ourcowerd with flouris laid in ane trane: 15
   All erdly joy returnis in pane.

'Come nevir ȝit May so fresche and grene,
Bot Januar come als wod and kene;
Wes nevir sic drowth bot anis come rane,
   All erdly joy returnis in pane.   20

'Evirmair unto this warldis joy
As nerrest air succeidis noy;
Thairfoir, quhen joy ma nocht remane,
   His verry air succeidis pane.

'Heir helth returnis in seiknes,   25
And mirth returnis in havines,
Toun in desert, forrest in plane;
   All erdly joy returnis in pane.

---

4 *returnis in*, turns into   6 *ass*, ash, dust   9 *eild*, age   15 *trane*, snare
18 *wod*, mad, fierce   22 *air*, heir   27 *plane*, treeless waste

'Fredome returnis in wrechitness,
And trewth returnis in dowbilness,   30
With fenȝeit wordis to mak men fane:
    All erdly joy returnis in pane.

'Vertew returnis in to vyce,
And honour in to avaryce;
With cuvatyce is consciens slane: 35
    All erdly joy returnis in pane.

'Sen erdly joy abydis nevir,
Wirk for the joy that lestis evir;
For uder joy is all bot vane:
    All erdly joy returnis in pane.'   40

31 *fenȝeit*, feigned

'Quhen He Wes Sek'

I that in heill wes and gladnes,
Am trublit now with gret seiknes
And feblit with infermite;
    Timor mortis conturbat me.

Our plesance heir is all vane glory,   5
This fals warld is bot transitory,
The flesch is brukle, the fend is sle;
    Timor mortis conturbat me.

The stait of man dois change and vary,
Now sound, now seik, now blith, now sary,   10
Now dansand mery, now like to dee;
    Timor mortis conturbat me.

No stait in erd heir standis sickir;
As with the wynd wavis the wickir
Wavis this warldis vanite;   15
    Timor mortis conturbat me.

On to the ded gois all estatis,
Princis, prelotis and potestatis,
Baith riche and pur of al degre;
    Timor mortis conturbat me.   20

He takis the knychtis in to the feild,
Enarmit undir helme and scheild;
Victour he is at all mellie;
    Timor mortis conturbat me.

1 *heill*, health   7 *brukle*, frail; *fend*, fiend; *sle*, cunning   10 *sary*, wretched
13 *sickir*, secure   14 *wickir*, willow   15 *vainte*, vanity   23 *mellie*, contest

That strang unmercifull tyrand   25
Takes on the moderis breist sowkand
The bab full of benignite;
Timor mortis conturbat me.

He takis the campion in the stour,
The capitane closit in the tour,   30
The lady in bour full of beaute;
Timor mortis conturbat me.

He sparis no lord for his piscence,
Na clerk for his intelligence;
His awfull strak may no man fle;   35
Timor mortis conturbat me.

Art magicianis and astrologgis,
Rethoris, logicianis and theologgis,
Thame helpis no conclusionis sle;
Timor mortis conturbat me.   40

In medicyne the most practicianis,
Lechis, surrigianis and phisicianis,
Thame self fra ded may not supple;
Timor mortis conturbat me.

I se that makaris amang the laif   45
Playis heir ther pageant, syne gois to graif;
Sparit is nought ther faculte;
Timor mortis conturbat me.

He hes done petuously devour
The noble Chaucer, of makaris flour,   50
The monk of Bery and Gower, all thre;
Timor mortis conturbat me.

---

29 *campion,* champion; *stour,* conflict   33 *piscence,* power   35 *strak,* stroke
38 *theologgis,* theologians   42 *lechis,* doctors; *surrigianis,* surgeons   43 *supple,*
deliver   45 *makaris,* poets; *laif,* rest

The gude Syr Hew of Eglintoun,
And eik Heryot and Wyntoun,
He has tane out of this cuntre;   55
    Timor mortis conturbat me.

That scorpion fell hes done infek
Maister Johne Clerk and James Afflek
Fra balat making and trigidie;
    Timor mortis conturbat me.   60

Holland and Barbour he hes berevit;
Allace! that he nought with us levit
Schir Mungo Lokert of the Le;
    Timor mortis conturbat me.

Clerk of Tranent eik he has tane,   65
That maid the anteris of Gawane;
Schir Gilbert Hay endit has he;
    Timor mortis conturbat me.

He has Blind Hary and Sandy Traill
Slaine with his schour of mortall haill,   70
Quhilk Patrik Johnestoun myght nought fle,
    Timor mortis conturbat me.

He hes reft Merseir his endite,
That did in luf so lifly write,
So schort, so quyk, of sentence hie;   75
    Timor mortis conturbat me.

He has tane Roull of Aberdene
And gentill Roull of Corstorphin;
Two bettir fallowis did no man se;
    Timor mortis conturbat me.   80

---

66 *anteris*, adventures   73 *endite*, writing   75 *sentence hie*, elevated thoughts

In Dunfermelyne he hes done roune
With Maister Robert Henrisoun;
Schir Johne the Ros enbrast has he;
   Timor mortis conturbat me.

And he hes now tane, last of aw,   85
Gud gentill Stobo and Quintyne Schaw,
Of quham all wichtis hes pete:
   Timor mortis conturbat me.

Gud Maister Walter Kennedy
In poynt of dede lyis veraly,   90
Gret reuth it wer that so suld be;
   Timor mortis conturbat me.

Sen he hes all my brether tane,
He will naught lat me lif alane,
On forse I man his nyxt pray be;   95
   Timor mortis conturbat me.

Sen for the deid remeid is none,
Best is that we for dede dispone,
Eftir our deid that lif may we;
   Timor mortis conturbat me.   100

81 *roune,* whisper   87 *wichtis,* men; *pete,* pity   91 *reuth,* pity   98 *dispone,*
make ready

Hale, sterne superne! Hale, in eterne,
  In Godis sicht to schyne!
Lucerne in derne for to discerne
  Be glory and grace devyne;
Hodiern, modern, sempitern,   5
  Angelicall regyne!
Our tern inferne for to dispern
  Helpe, rialist rosyne.
    Ave Maria, gracia plena!
Haile, fresche floure femynyne!   10
3erne us guberne, virgin matern,
  Of reuth baith rute and ryne.

Haile, 3hing, benyng, fresche flurising!
  Haile, Alphais habitakle!
Thy dyng ofspring maid us to syng   15
  Befor his tabernakle;
All thing maling we doune thring,
  Be sicht of his signakle;
Quhilk king us bring unto his ryng,
  Fro dethis dirk umbrakle.   20
    Ave Maria, gracia plena!
Haile, moder and maide but makle!
Bricht syng, gladyng our languissing,
  Be micht of thi mirakle.

1 *sterne superne*, divine star   3 *lucerne in derne*, light in darkness
5 *hodiern*, of today   7 *tern*, gloom; *dispern*, disperse   8 *rialist*, most royal
11 *3erne*, swiftly; *guberne*, guide   12 *reuth*, pity; *ryne*, bark   13 *3hing*, young
14 *habitakle*, habitation   15 *dyng*, worthy   17 *doune thring*, overthrow
18 *signakle*, sign   19 *ryng*, reign   20 *umbrakle*, shades   22 *but makle*, spotless

Haile, bricht be sicht in hevyn on hicht! 25
   Haile, day sterne orientale!
Our licht most richt, in clud of nycht,
   Our dirknes for to scale:
Hale, wicht in ficht, puttar to flicht
   Of fendis in battale! 30
Haile, plicht but sicht! Hale, mekle of mycht!
   Haile, glorius Virgin, hale!
    Ave Maria, gracia plena!
   Haile, gentill nychttingale!
Way stricht, cler dicht, to wilsome wicht, 35
   That irke bene in travale.

Hale, qwene serene! Hale, most amene!
   Haile, hevinlie hie emprys!
Haile, schene unseyne with carnale eyne!
   Haile, ros of paradys! 40
Haile, clene bedene, ay till conteyne!
   Haile, fair fresche flour delyce!
Haile, grene daseyne! Haile, fro the splene
   Of Jhesu genetrice!
    Ave Maria, gracia plena! 45
   Thow baire the prince of prys;
Our teyne to meyne, and ga betweyne
   As humile oratrice.

28 *scale*, disperse   29 *wicht*, strong   31 *plicht*, main anchor; *but sicht*, unseen
35 *cler dicht*, fairly prepared; *wilsome*, wandering   36 *irke*, weary   37 *amene*,
delightful   39 *schene*, fair   41 *clene*, pure; *bedene*, completely; *conteyne*, endure
42 *flour delyce*, lily   43 *daseyne*, daisy; *fro the splene*, from the heart   47 *teyne*,
affliction; *meyne*, pity   48 *oratrice*, intercessor

Haile, more decore than of before,
    And swetar be sic sevyne,   50
Our glore forlore for to restore,
    Sen thow art qwene of hevyn!
Memore of sore, stern in Aurore,
    Lovit with angellis stevyne;
Implore, adore, thow indeflore,   55
    To mak our oddis evyne.
        Ave Maria, gracia plena!
    With lovingis lowde ellevyn.
Quhill store and hore my ȝouth devore,
    Thy name I sall ay nevyne.   60

Empryce of prys, imperatrice,
    Brycht polist precious stane;
Victrice of vyce, hie genetrice
    Of Jhesu, lord soverayne:
Our wys pavys fro enemys,   65
    Agane the feyndis trayne;
Oratrice, mediatrice, salvatrice,
    To God gret suffragane!
        Ave Maria, gracia plena!
    Haile, sterne meridiane!   70
Spyce, flour delice of paradys,
    That baire the gloryus grayne.

Imperiall wall, place palestrall,
    Of peirless pulcritud;
Tryumphale hall, hie trone regall   75
    Of Godis celsitud;
Hospitall riall, the lord of all
    Thy closet did include;
Bricht ball cristall, ros virginall,
    Fulfillit of angell fude.   80
        Ave Maria, gracia plena!
    Thy birth has with his blude
Fra fall mortall originall
    Us raunsound on the rude.

49 *decore*, beautiful   50 *be sic sevyne*, sevenfold   53 *memore*, reminder; *sore*, pain
54 *lovit*, praised; *stevyne*, voices   55 *indeflore*, virgin   58 *lovingis*, praises
59 *store and hore*, struggle and age   60 *nevyne*, invoke   65 *pavys*, shield
66 *trayne*, trick   68 *suffragane*, assistant   73 *palestrall*, magnificent   76 *celsitud*,
majesty   77 *hospitall*, lodging   78 *include*, contain   84 *raunsound*, ransomed

Rorate celi desuper!
Hevins distill ʒour balmy schouris,
For now is rissin the bricht day ster
Fro the ros Mary, flour of flouris;
The cleir sone quhome no clud devouris,   5
Surminting Phebus in the est,
Is cumin of his hevinly touris
Et nobis Puer natus est.

Archangellis, angellis and dompnationis,
Tronis, potestatis and marteiris seir,   10
And all ʒe hevinly operationis,
Ster, planeit, firmament and speir,
Fyre, erd, air and watter cleir
To him give loving, most and lest,
That come in to so meik maneir,   15
Et nobis Puer natus est.

Synnaris be glaid and pennance do
And thank ʒour Makar hairtfully,
For he that ʒe mycht nocht cum to
To ʒow is cumin full humly,   20
ʒour saulis with his blud to by
And lous ʒow of the feindis arrest,
And only of his awin mercy;
Pro nobis Puer natus est.

All clergy do to him inclyne   25
And bow unto that barne benyng,
And do ʒour observance devyne
To him that is of kingis King;
Ensence his alter, reid and sing
In haly kirk with mynd degest,   30
Him honouring attour all thing,
Qui nobis Puer natus est.

10 *seir*, various   12 *speir*, sphere   14 *loving*, praise   22 *lous*, loose   30
degest, settled   31 *attour*, above

Celestiall fowlis in the are
Sing with ȝour nottis upoun hicht,
In firthis and in forrestis fair   35
Be myrthfull now, at all ȝour mycht,
For passit is ȝour dully nycht,
Aurora hes the cluddis perst,
The son is rissin with glaidsum lycht
Et nobis Puer natus est.   40

Now spring up flouris fra the rute,
Revert ȝow upwart naturaly
In honour of the blissit frute
That rais up from the rose Mary;
Lay out ȝour levis lustely,   45
Fro deid tak lyfe now at the lest
In wirschip of that Prince wirthy,
Qui nobis Puer natus est.

Syng hevin imperiall, most of hicht,
Regions of air mak armony;   50
All fishe in flud and foull of flicht
Be myrthfull, and mak melody:
All Gloria in excelsis cry,
Hevin, erd, se, man, bird and best,
He that is crownit abone the sky   55
Pro nobis Puer natus est.

35 *firthis*, woods   37 *dully*, dreary   42 *revert*, spring up again

Done is a battell on the dragon blak,
Our campioun Chryst confountet hes his force;
The ʒettis of hell ar brokin with a crak,
The signe triumphall rasit is of the croce;
The divillis trymmillis with hiddous voce,   5
The saulis ar borrowit and to the blis can go,
Chryst with his blud our ransonis dois indoce:
Surrexit Dominus de sepulchro.

Dungin is the deidly dragon Lucifer,
The crewall serpent with the mortall stang;   10
The auld kene tegir with his teith on char
Quhilk in a wait hes lyne for us so lang,
Thinking to grip us in his clows strang;
The mercifull Lord wald nocht that it wer so,
He maid him for to felʒe of that fang: 15
Surrexit Dominus de sepulchro.

He for our saik that sufferit to be slane
And lyk a lamb in sacrifice wes dicht,
Is lyk a lyone rissin up agane
And as [a] gyane raxit him on hicht;   20
Sprungin is Aurora radius and bricht,
On loft is gone the glorius Appollo,
The blisfull day depairtit from the nycht:
Surrexit Dominus de sepulchro.

The grit victour agane is rissin on hicht,   25
That for our querrell to the deth wes woundit;
The sone that wox all paill now schynis bricht,
And dirknes clerit, our fayth is now refoundit;
The knell of mercy fra the hevin is soundit,
The Cristin ar deliverit of thair wo,   30
The Jowis and thair errour ar confoundit:
Surrexit Dominus de sepulchro.

---

2 *force*, strength   3 *ʒettis*, gates   5 *trymmillis*, tremble   6 *borrowit*, redeemed
7 *indoce*, endorse   9 *dungin*, cast down   11 *on char*, slightly open   15 *felʒe*,
fall short; *fang*, prey   18 *dicht*, made ready   31 *Jowis*, Jews

The fo is chasit, the battell is done ceis,
The presone brokin, the jevellouris fleit and flemit;
The weir is gon, confermit is the peis, 35
The fetteris lowsit and the dungeoun temit,
The ransoun maid, the presoneris redemit;
The feild is win, ourcumin is the fo,
Dispulit of the tresur that he ʒemit:
Surrexit Dominus de sepulchro. 40

34 *jevellouris*, jailors; *flemit*, put to flight   36 *temit*, emptied   39 ʒ*emit*, guarded

NOTES

In all cases, the first source listed is that used.

1. DUNBAR AT OXINFURDE (M)
The colophon to the Maitland text, 'Quod Dumbar at oxinfurde', is the
only authority for attributing this poem to Dunbar, and the only indica-
tion that he ever visited Oxford. The date 1501 has been suggested for
the poem on the basis that Dunbar is believed to have been in England
in that year, and, if correct, would make this an early composition. The
stanza form, which derives from French originals, was one which he was
to use again with great effect, most notably in no. 36.
11   *The naturall science*: the study of natural phenomena

2. THE THRISSEL AND THE ROIS (B)
The marriage of James IV to Henry VII's daughter Margaret was under
negotiation from 1495 until January 1502, when a proxy marriage took
place. The real marriage did not take place until 1503 when Margaret,
then thirteen years old, set out for Scotland in July. This poem, which
celebrates the marriage, might therefore have been written in 1502 after
the proxy marriage but should more likely be dated 9 May 1503 (the day
is noted in the final line) when the preparations for Margaret's arrival
and state wedding in Scotland were being made. Caution, however,
should be used in accepting this dating too literally; see Bawcutt, pp.
74–5. The stanza is the French *chant-royal*, used by Chaucer in *Troilus and
Criseyde* and by James I in *The Kingis Quair* (from which its English name
of Rime Royal is erroneously supposed to derive).
5   *begyn thair houris*: the services of the church were referred to as
      'hours', from the set hours at which they were held (cp. 'Book of
      Hours' for a service book). The service here would most probably
      be Prime, which was sung at 6 a.m., since Matins was normally
      sung at midnight.
9   *Aurora*: goddess of dawn
33   *Eolus*: in classical mythology the keeper of the winds
46   *eftir hir*: an emendation introduced by Allan Ramsay in his printing
      in *The Evergreen* (1724). B: *full haistely*
64   *Dame Nature*: for the rather curious origins of the goddess Nature,
      as she appears in medieval literature, see C..S. Lewis, *The Discarded
      Image*, chap. 3.
65   *Neptunus*: god of the seas
69   *Juno*: in Roman mythology the wife of Jupiter and the goddess
      primarily associated with women and marriage.
96–8 The description of the red Lion of Scotland (James IV) rampant on

a golden field within a border decorated with fleurs de lys is an exact description of the heraldic beast on the royal coat of arms. James is shown in turn as the lion, king of beasts, the eagle, king of birds and finally the thistle, the emblem of Scotland, king of flowers, the form in which he appears in the title of the poem.

119   *parcere prostratis*: 'to pardon those who prostrate themselves', a quotation from the motto frequently associated with the royal Scottish arms, *parcere prostratis scit nobilis ira leonis*, deriving from Pliny, *Natural History*, viii, 19. In heraldic symbolism the lion represented majesty, mercy and watchfulness.

122   *awppis*: bullfinches. Bawcutt suggests an error for 'quhawppis' (curlew), an uglier bird than the bullfinch.

129–30   Bawcutt (p. 100) points out how recently the thistle had been adopted as the Scottish symbol

135–40   A reminder to the notoriously philandering king to confine himself in future to his bride.

142   *reid and quhyt*: Margaret was the child of the union between the red rose of Lancaster (Henry VII) and the white rose of York (Elizabeth Plantagenet). See also line 171.

180   *perle*: the queen's name in Latin ('margarita') means 'pearl'.

3.   ON HIS HEID-AKE (R)

6   *schir*: James IV

4.   HOW DUMBAR WAS DESYRD TO BE ANE FREIR (B, M, R)

It has been suggested on the basis of this poem that Dunbar had once been a friar (see Introduction, p. xii) but the poem is better read as a standard satire on the immorality of friars, and on the appropriateness that the fiend should take this shape to tempt the poet, only to vanish in a puff of smoke when resisted. Simpson Ross (p. 196) has pointed out the neat parodic reversal of the conventional idea of the angel presenting a Franciscan habit to St Francis, as illustrated in the basilica at Assisi.

1   The poem's setting in a nightmare, rather than a dream, seems a reversal of the conventional medieval dream setting as used in, for example, no. 2. But the *visum* or *phantasm* which included nightmare was also a recognised literary form.

21   *allevin*: normally 'eleven' but that seems unlikely here, particularly followed by the multiple of seven in the next line. Possibly a line-filler such as 'all in all'.

34   *Kalice*: Calais (at this time part of England)

38   *Derntoun*: Darlington, Co. Durham

5.   COMPLAINT TO THE KING AGANIS MURE (M, R)

This may well be the first literary copyright complaint on record. The identity of Mure (presumably a rival but inferior poet) is not known. The complaint reveals both Dunbar's pride in his own ability and his fear (possibly not as jocular as it seems here) that the slander and treason written by Mure in Dunbar's name might be ascribed to him.

6   *hyne to Calis*: from here to Calais, then an English possession (a

proverbial expression)

19   *rowndit heid*: cropped head, a form of punishment

24   *Cuddy Rug*: it is recorded (LHTA, II, 457) that a fool called Cuddy performed before the king in Dumfries in September 1504, where he stole a drum from a drummer. His name recurs up to 1512.

26   ȝ*allow and reid*: the colours of the royal livery, but also the colours worn by court jesters

6.   ANE HIS AWIN ENNEMY (B, M)

This stanza (aabab) with the fifth line a refrain, was one of Dunbar's favourites, and is used frequently, often (though not exclusively) for poems of morality. Dunbar turns with skill from stereotyped misfortune (for example, 'ane wicket wyfe') to his own particular misfortune (service to a master 'that nevir of him will haif no rewth').

14   *fleis of Spenȝie*: syphilis (which Alexander Montgomerie later wished on his opponent, Polwarth, in their flyting); but the term was also used for a sexual stimulant.

7.   THE FLYTING OF DUNBAR AND KENNEDIE (B, C&M, M)

This is the earliest known example in Scots or English of the flyting, a peculiarly Scottish literary form. Subsequent exemplars are the flytings between James V and Sir David Lyndsay of the Mount and between Alexander Montgomerie and Sir Patrick Hume of Polwarth. The origins of the flyting have been traced back to the Greek *agon*, the Provençal *tenson*, medieval debates and contentions and even to Gaelic contests of bardic wit. W.P. Ker described it as '*Vetus Comoedia*, a debate or contest, all made up of railing accusations. The origin is everywhere, the amusement is known to Greeks and Barbarians, and it is developed in different countries into different literary forms.' The hallmarks of the genre, as it developed in Scotland, were its gusto and its scurrility. There may not have been (probably was not) any real antagonism between the opponents in what has been described as a 'miracle of ... literary Billingsgate' (Baildon, p. 259). Kennedy was later to be described by Dunbar in the 'Lament for the Makaris' (33) as 'gud Maister Walter Kennedy', and is referred to respectfully in the poems of Lyndsay and Douglas.

The flyting was a poetic contest, probably recited before the king, to establish who was the better poet. Montgomerie beat Polwarth; Lyndsay was undoubtedly too skilful a courtier to beat his master, James V; it is not recorded whether Dunbar or his opponent, Walter Kennedy was the winner, but the reader is invited before Dunbar's final attack on Kennedy to 'juge in the nixt quha gat the war'.

Walter Kennedy was the third son of Gilbert, 1st Lord Kennedy of Dunure and grandson of Mary, Countess of Angus, a daughter of Robert III (hence his claim in line 417, 'I am the kingis blude'). He was also nephew of the Bishop of Dunkeld and St Andrews and uncle of David Kennedy, later Earl of Cassillis and privy councillor to James IV. He was, in fact, extremely well connected, almost certainly more so than Dunbar.

The poem has been assumed on slender internal evidence to have been written between 1500 and 1505. The earlier date is the more probable.

The stanza, also known as the French octave and not used by Dunbar elsewhere, rhymes ababbccb with the addition of four-stress alliteration and, in each poet's closing piece, a torrent of internal rhyme. This was to be regarded in future as the conventional flyting stanza. Space forbids the printing of the whole exchange, but all Dunbar's contributions are given, and Kennedy's first for purposes of comparison.

1–2   In this contest each poet was supported by a second or 'commissar'. Dunbar's 'Sir John the Ross' has been tentatively identified as Sir John the Ross of Hawkhead (d. 1500–1) who appears later in no. 31. Walter Kennedy was supported by his cousin Quintin, of whom little is known.

7   *Lucifer*: the morning star, identified with Satan, the archangel thrown from heaven for rebelling against God.

17   *baird*: Kennedy was of Highland birth (was Gaelic-speaking), hence the disparaging description of him as an Irish ('Ersche') bard, a practitioner demonstrably inferior to a makar (cp. line 49).

29   *maid maister bot in mows*: 'made a master of arts in jest'

43   *werlot of the cairtis*: 'knave of cards' (Kinsley) but more likely a menial who loads and unloads carts

77–8   This has been taken as an allusion to a conspiracy by the Earl of Lennox and Lord Lyle against James IV in 1489, when the royal forces attacked both conspirators' Renfrewshire castles. It is improbable that the Kennedys were involved in the plot.

83   *glengoir loun* (B): M has 'Ganʒelon' or Ganelon, the traitor of the *Chanson de Roland*.

89–96   These lines have been taken as evidence of Dunbar's overseas travels. There has been argument as to whether 'Seland' means the Zeeland of the Low Countries (with which Scotland had extensive trading connections) or the Danish Zealand. Either would fit.

110–12   'I'll wager that a Lothian arse can produce better and more perfect English than you can blabber with your Carrick lips'. Lowland Scots was generally described as 'Inglis' to differentiate it from 'Ersche' or Gaelic.

123   *Lawarance*: St Lawrence or Laurentius, martyred at Rome in the persecutions of Valerianus by being roasted on a gridiron.

124   *Sanct Johnis ene*: probably John the Baptist, who is shown in medieval paintings as blindfolded before he was decapitated. St John the Apostle is said to have died in his bed, and St John Chrysostom died of natural causes.

125   *St Augustine of Canterbury* is reported in Fordun's *Scotichronicon* to have been struck 'with skaitt rumpillis' (fish tails) by unconverted English who disliked his preaching. Hence the vengeance of God condemned the English to wear tails.

126   *Bartilmo*: said to have been flayed alive before his crucifixion.

131   *kis his erss*: in the Black Mass, disciples were supposed to kiss the Devil's backside.

134   *Karrik*, like Galloway in line 141, is used to describe the Celtic south-west corner of Scotland, from which the Kennedy family came.

145   *Katherene*: cateran, a Highland reiver or robber

161   *Lazarus*: not the leper, the resurrected corpse
169   *lukis*: M has *linkis*, joints.
172   *spreit of Gy*: the spirit of Guido de Corvo, who was so persistent in
       haunting his wife that it took four Dominican friars to restrain and
       exorcise him. The story (which is told in *Scotichronicon*, xiii, 609) is
       referred to also in 'Ane litill interlud of the droichis part of the play'
       (B), one of the reasons for ascribing this anonymous fragment to
       Dunbar.
191   *sawsy in saphron*: 'steeped in a saffron sauce'; saffron was a specific
       for gouty and rheumatic complaints.
192   *prymros*: its properties are antispasmodic, vermifuge, emetic and
       astringent. The powdered root is referred to by Pliny as an impor-
       tant remedy for muscular rheumatism, paralysis and gout. An
       infusion of the flowers is 'famous for curing the phrensie' (Gerard),
       but it is clearly the powdered root that is meant here.
197   *to me* (MF); B: *to my*
209   *Strait Gibbonis air*: Kinsley notes a payment made in 1503 to 'Strait
       Gibbon' (possibly a court jester) by royal command.
233   *Mahoun*: Mahomet, in the Middle Ages a false god or devil
241   *Hilhous*: 'an obscure allusion to Sir John Sandilands of Hillhouse,
       near Edinburgh' (Kinsley)

8.   MEDITATIOUN IN WYNTIR (M, R)
There is no internal evidence to date this beautiful meditation, but it
seems the poetry of an elderly man. The ideas expressed are common to
much medieval poetry, but here are given a personal and regional appli-
cation. The isometrical tail-rhyme stanza (aabab) is one Dunbar uses
most frequently (see no. 6, note, above).
3   'A troublesome tempestuous air is as bad as impure, rough and
      foul weather, impetuous winds, cloudy dark days, as it is
      commonly with us . . . And who is not weather-wise against such
      and such conjunction of Planets, moved in foul weather, dull and
      heavy in such tempestuous seasons?' (Burton, *Anatomy of
      Melancholy*, I, 2, ii, 5).
17   *Despair*, in the Catholic Church, is a sin against hope, since by
      despair a man ceases to look for salvation from God. In addition to
      the canonical sin, however, Dunbar is despairing of his poor
      prospects and lack of money and the imminence of old age and ill
      health.
25   *glas*: the hourglass of Fortune, symbol of the transience of life and
      prosperity.
36–7 'Then Death throws open his wide gates, saying "These shall wait
      open for thee".'

9–11. OF DISCRETIOUN IN ASKING, OF DISCRETIOUN IN GEVING, OF
      DISCRETIOUN IN TAKING (B, M, R)
This group of three poems, which in the Maitland MS appear as a single
poem, are closely allied in temper and approach and exemplify Dunbar's
skill in taking conventional forms of morality and turning them into

something fresh and individual by his application of the general to the particular. Discretion had a stronger sense in Dunbar's day than in ours, closer to the faculty of reason. The social criticism becomes more biting through the succession of poems.

Of Discretioun in Asking
13 'Some are ashamed to ask, as is my nature'. This may have been a joke since there is little evidence that Dunbar was ever ashamed to ask.
17 'It's no blame to ask for reward for service'
38 'Because he can't wait for the right moment'.

Of Discretioun in Geving
3–4 Dunbar's anger at the gift of benefices and other rewards to those already adequately supplied at the expense of those (like himself) who have nothing is a recurring theme (see also lines 31–4).
17 'Until the asker is so tired'
36–7 *strangeris...fra Flanderis*: generally supposed to be a reference to Damian, Abbot of Tungland (see The 'Fenȝeit Freir of Tungland', no. 22) who came high on Dunbar's list of undeserving beneficiaries; if so, it would probably date these poems around 1504, the date at which he received his abbacy.
49 'There are many such nowadays'
51 *gud kewis*: some editors have discarded B's 'gud' as accidental repetition from earlier in the line. *Kewis* is the theatrical sense of 'cue'; that is, for giving the right answers.

Of Discretioun in Taking
Dunbar plays throughout on the difference between 'taking' (receiving) and 'taking' (taking by force, pillaging, thieving). M contains 2 stanzas missing in B, given here in [   ].
13 *mailis*: usually rents paid in money rather than in kind; *gersomes*: rents paid in advance for a lease of more than a year.
48–9 'Poor takers are hanged high and are shamed forever, with their descendants'

12. REMONSTRANCE TO THE KING (M)
This poem rises above the somewhat hackneyed medieval catalogue format through the genuine passion and anger which inform it. In it, Dunbar pleads for the greater discretion in giving ('for mereit and for meidis') of which he finds so little in no. 10 and flytes at the 'fenȝeouris, fleichouris and flatteraris' who are rewarded by the king at the expense of his more profitable servants. The most memorable part is his claim for the merits of his own work in lines 25–34, and the ringing reminder in the closing lines that a king fails to reward a poet at his own peril. The description of the worthy and unworthy servants provides a vivid picture of the social life of Edinburgh at the time and of the king's own interests and preoccupations. Many of the references in this poem can be confirmed from the description of James's court (dated 25 July 1498) by

114

the Spanish Ambassador, Don Pedro de Ayala, a translation of which is printed in P. Hume Brown's *Early Travellers in Scotland* (Edinburgh, 1891). The Treasurer's accounts amply bear out Dunbar's accusations of royal extravagance.

10   Maitland has left a blank in the line here, though in fact no further word is actually required by the scansion.

16   *Pryntouris*: a reminder that James IV licensed the first Scottish printers, Walter Chepman and Androw Myllar, to establish their press in Edinburgh in 1507. Six of Dunbar's poems (seven, if 'Kynd Kittok' is correctly attributed to him) appeared among their earliest publications in 1508. This reference would date this poem after 1507.

55   *ingynouris*: this may be another hit at Damian, the 'fenʒeit freir of Tungland (see no. 22). Damian claimed to have the quintessence that would turn base metal into gold.

66   *Cokelbeis gryce*: Dunbar compares the undeserving claimants with the very similar rabble who assembled to eat the little pig in *The Tale of Colkelbie's Sow* (ed. Gregory Kratzmann, New York and London, 1983).

13.   TO THE KING THAT HE WAR JOHNE THOMSOUNIS MAN (M)
Joan or John Thomson's husband was totally subservient to his wife; in this lively and amusing appeal, Dunbar wishes that the king were John Thomson's man, since he would then listen to the queen's recommendations on Dunbar's behalf. His pleas for advancement are combined with praise of Queen Margaret; there are several indications in Dunbar's poetry that he was closer to the young queen than to the king.

19   It was the chivalric custom for kings and princes to vow important undertakings on the swan or the peacock, both royal birds.

21–2 Dunbar's reference here to the Thistle and the Rose is probably intended to remind the king of his wedding poem (no. 2) and reward due for it.

31   *Sanct An*: St Anne, mother of the Virgin Mary

14.   TO THE LORDIS OF THE KINGIS CHALKER (R)
Another humorous appeal for financial relief, this time to the Lords of Exchequer who audited the royal revenues.

11   The Lord Treasurer was responsible for the payment of Dunbar's pension.

15.   TO THE KING (M, B)
This appeal to the king, again in Dunbar's favourite aabab tail-rhyme stanza, enlarges in a more meditative way on his financial straits, and on the whole system of just reward for service touched on in other poems. Like no. 8, it is the complaint of a man facing the hardship of old age without money or position.

1   ʒe: *yit* (B)

11–12 The reward of low-born inferiors at the expense of men of good family who had better deserved promotion (an offence against the medieval concept of degree, cp. line 39) is a recurring theme.

7   *rid halk*: red merlin (Kinsley); young hawk, that is, with red plumage (Bawcutt)

18   *the corchet cleiff*: hit the note (crotchet) in the centre

21   *farrest foulis*: birds from furthest away, possibly another hit at Damian, the abbot of Tungland (no. 22).

26   *egill*: Dunbar addresses the king as the eagle, king of birds, in no. 2.

33   *Raf Coilȝear ... Johnne the Reif*: Rauf Coilyear (Ralph the Collier) is the rough, unmannered hero of an early Scottish romance, who rescues Charlemagne in a snowstorm but, not knowing who he is, treats him disrespectfully. John the Reif (reeve) is the equally low-born hero of a similar English ballad, which was clearly well known in Scotland since Douglas, like Dunbar, brackets the two in his *Palice of Honour*:

> I saw Rauf Colzear with his thrawin brow
> Crabit John the Reif and auld Cowkellpis sow.

61–2 These lines have been read as implying that Dunbar had been bred to the church, even brought up to expect a bishopric. But it has been pointed out by Kinsley that 'dandillie, bischop, dandillie' might be a quotation from a nursery song.

64   *vicar*: a deputy, one who does the duty of a parish for an incumbent who draws the revenues, one of the lowest forms of beneficed clerics.

72   *dispensationis*: papal dispensations to hold several livings at once

74   *totum... nychell*: 'He gets everything, I get nothing.' In a game of chance, 'a totum was a four-sided disk made for a spinning toy, with a letter inscribed on each side: T (*totum*), A (*aufer*), D (*depone*), N (*nihil*, "*nichell*"), the player's fortune being set by the letter uppermost when the toy fell' (Kinsley, p. 320).

16.   IN THIS WARLD MAY NONE ASSURE (M, B, R)

Although the framework of this poem is religious ('Lord' in line 6 changes by line 81 from the King to God), the inspiration is not: the ending is conventionally pious but the recurring complaint is of social injustice and the themes explored in no. 15. The economy and effectiveness of the imagery is particularly striking, as in lines 36–8 and 46–50. The refrain is a variant on a proverbial saying.

28   'Freedom is forfeited'; this is legal terminology.

49   *laith to dispone*: 'reluctant to give'

63   *bugill sture*: the last trumpet

71–2 *Ube... Ve!*: 'Where the burning souls shall continually cry "Woe, Woe!"' The Latin in this stanza comes from the Office of the Dead.

74   *O quante... tenebre*: 'How great is that darkness?'

82   *De terra... sum*: 'I shall have risen from the earth'

84   *in regnum tuum*: 'in thy kingdom'

17. THE PETITION OF THE GRAY HORSE, AULD DUNBAR (M, R)
This, one of Dunbar's best-known poems, is a more humorous and witty plea to the King for relief. The fact that it is written in the form of a carol fits the fact that this was a Christmas appeal. It would be interesting to know whether the King's response was written by James (who was clearly capable of doing so) or by Dunbar himself, as a hint of what reply was expected – though if Dunbar had written it, he would probably have kept to the stanza of the main poem.

2   3owllis 3ald: Kinsley points out the special use of 3ald, normally an old horse, to describe someone not wearing a new garment at Christmas; it has survived in north-east Scotland in, for example, 'paseyad', someone with nothing new to wear for Easter. Payments to Dunbar for his Christmas gown in 1505 and 1506 are recorded in LHTA.

5   Strenever: Strathnaver, in Sutherland, about the most remote and barren part of Scotland

30   evill schoud: the meaning is obscure. Scott (p. 110) offers 'badly-cleaned' but provides no evidence for this interpretation.

33   my thrift be thyne: 'I spend more than I save'

45   lufferis: this has generally been glossed 'lovers'; but Bawcutt (2, p. 449) points out that it can also mean 'livery' in the double sense of clothing for courtiers and provisions for horses, and this makes much better sense.

18. A BRASH OF WOWING (M, B, R)
This is a burlesque of the traditional medieval chanson d'aventure, a love encounter overheard by an eavesdropper. But in this case, instead of the flowery rhetoric of the usual amour courtois lovers, Dunbar follows the traditional opening with a rather more robust situation. The technique is similar to the one he was to use (or may already have used, since neither piece can be precisely dated) in no. 27. In contrast to the Tretis, however, this is a straightforward piece of earthy ribaldry, the language starting with the terms of a traditional love complaint and then rapidly degenerating. It is untitled in all sources, this title having been invented by Allan Ramsay.

6   danger: the significance of 'danger' in courtly love differs from contemporary usage. Lewis derives it from 'Dominus through Dominarium; and from the meaning of "lordship" and "lordliness" all its other semantic history can be explained. I can well see how a word of this origin could acquire the sense of "haughtiness" or, in our modern colloquial language, "stand-offishness", or "difficulty in granting"' (Allegory of Love, p. 124). Here, the girl is being accused of being stand-offish.

17   'I never wooed anyone but you'

23   tuchan: B has Cowffyne which is obscure. A tuchan was a stuffed calf-skin, used to encourage a cow to give milk, which would make perfectly good sense here if it were not for the tautological 'calfe' which follows.

28   'I dearly love your ugly mug'

117

33 *hals*: this is a reading from B, and has been adopted as preferable. M has *heilis*, which makes much less sense. Ladies' necks were frequently praised by medieval lovers, heels rarely.

44 *bryl3oun*: '?pudendum muliebre' (Kinsley). Bawcutt suggests an error for *ryl3oun*, a shoe of undressed hide, which goes better with 'ruch' (rough, hairy).

51 *golk of Marie land*: an allusion to the old ballad of *King Berdok*, who wooed Mayok, the 'golk in Maryland'. The ballad is found in the Bannatyne MS and printed by David Laing in his *Early Popular Poetry of Scotland* (Edinburgh, 1884). Maryland has nothing to do with the Virgin, 'Marie' deriving from OE *mere* or *mera*, a goblin or malicious fairy. The word survives in 'nightmare'.

19. OF A DANCE IN THE QUENIS CHALMER (M)

This account of an evening in the queen's chambers, possibly written at her request to commemorate a particular occasion, is a happy and intimate portrait of the other side of Dunbar's life at court, and can be set in apposition to the numerous other occasions in which he portrays himself standing excluded at the door.

1 *Sir Jhon Sinclair*: Sir John Sinclair of Dryden, one of the officials who took part (as did Dunbar himself) in the mission to negotiate the marriage of James IV and Margaret Tudor in 1501. His name appears frequently in court accounts and records. On this occasion, he had presumably just returned from another mission to France. Several critics have pointed out that the staggering metre of the poem in most verses mimics the ungraceful gait of the dancers; only in the stanzas describing the dancing of Mistress Musgrave and Dunbar himself does it flow more smoothly.

8 *Maistir Robert Scha*: Shaw has been identified with a court physician whose name appears in the records 1502–8 and who may have taken orders in 1508.

15 *the Maister Almaser*: Kinsley suggests that this may have been the Englishman Dr Babington, who came to Scotland with the queen, remained as her almoner and was later Dean of Aberdeen. He had died by May 1507; but, as Bawcutt points out, the office would continue after Babington's death, and this reference could be either to his successor or, even more likely, the king's almoner (Bawcutt, pp. 50–1).

19 *John Bute*: a court fool who first appears in the *LHTA* records in November 1506. There are descriptions of the rich coloured clothing ordered for him.

29 *maesteress Musgraeffe*: probably the wife of Sir John Musgrave, and one of the queen's ladies.

36 *Dame Dounteboir*: a derogatory term for an elderly court lady. Cp. Knox's *History of the Reformation*: 'old dountybowris ... that long had served in the Court'.

44 *The Quenis dog*: probably her wardrober, James Dog (see no. 20 below).

47 'How like a cur he pranced about'

20. OF JAMES DOG, KEPAIR OF THE QUENIS WARDREP (M)
According to Kinsley, who bases his note on *LHTA*, 'this and [no. 21] concern Dunbar's attempt (ultimately successful) to get a doublet out of the keeper of the queen's wardrobe. James Dog had been groom of the king's wardrobe.... He passed into the queen's service in a position of great responsibility, with the charge of furnishings, tapestries, and the like as well as liveries, and with control of payments in kind to court servants. He evidently remained in this post at least until 1527'. As in the previous poem, the humour consists in Dunbar's attribution to the unfortunate Dog (or Doig) of canine characteristics.

2–3 *he is... syd frog*: 'he makes as much fuss as if he were being asked for a full length cloak'.

10 *that*: 'so that'

19 *the grytt Sowdan Gog-ma-gog*: a Sowdane is a Muslim Sultan, hence any pagan king. Gog-ma-Gog, according to Geoffrey of Monmouth (*Historia Regum Brittaniae*, trans. Lewis Thorpe, 1969, pp. 53–4), was one of the giants of Albion, thrown into the sea off Cornwall by one of the Trojan followers of Brutus.

23 'His gait makes all your chamber shake'

21. OF THE SAID JAMES, QUHEN HE HAD PLESETT HIM (M)
Dunbar has got his doublet. John Pinkerton (*Ancient Scotish Poems*, 1786, ii, 409) queries 'whether was it most dangerous to displease, or to please Dunbar?' Kinsley (p. 304) notes that there actually was a James Lam at court, as well as a James Doig.

13–20 It is not clear whether Doig actually had a wife who had (or did not have) these characteristics or whether Dunbar was hypothetically imagining such a misfortune.

22. THE FEN3EIT FREIR OF TUNGLAND (B, A)
James IV's interest in scientific experiment, particularly in new ideas in medicine and surgery, made him vulnerable to cranks and quacks, of whom Damian was a notable example. John Damian de Falcusis, described variously as of French or Italian origin, arrived in Scotland some time between 1501 and 1504 when (to Dunbar's fury) he was made Abbot of Tungland in Galloway, and secured James's patronage for his alchemical experiments. Having failed in his efforts to discover the quintessence which would enable him to turn base metal into gold, he attempted to revive the king's flagging interest by trying to fly to France from the ramparts of Stirling Castle with wings made of birds' feathers. The experiment is described by Bishop John Lesley (trans. James Dalrymple, *History of Scotland*, Bannatyne Club, 1830, p. 76):

> To baith his schouders he couples his wings, that of dyvers foulis he had prouydet, fra the hicht of the castel of Sterling as he wald tak Jornay, he makis him to flie up in the air; bot or he was weil begun, his veyage was at an end, for this deceiuer fel doun with sik a dade, that the bystanders wist not, quhither tha sulde mair meine his dolour, or meruel of his dafrie. Al rinis to visit him, tha ask the

Abbot with his wings how he did. He answers that his thich bane is brokne, and he hopet neuer to gang agane.

Seeing himself 'in sik derisioun', he made the excuse that he should have stuck to eagle feathers: 'thair was sum hen fedderis in the wingis, quhilk yarnit and covet the midding [midden] and not the skyis'. The episode provided Dunbar with rich material for satire, and he made the most of it, both in this poem and in 'The Antechrist' ('Lucina schynning in silence of the nicht'). In 'The Fenȝeit Freir', he starts from the conventional dream opening in a happy dancing measure which expresses better than anything else could do his zest in ridiculing Damian as incompetent (and murderous) leech, corrupt cleric and unsuccessful aviator. It should be noted that Lesley wrote many years after the events described here; for a more sceptical view of the authenticity of this episode, see Bawcutt, pp. 57–8.

3 B's 'swenyng' is probably an error for A's 'swewyng', a vision or dream.

5 There is no evidence that Damian came from Turkey. Dunbar simply implies that he is a Muslim, an infidel, hence 'a son of Satan', who comes from barbarian parts ('boundis of Barbary'). See also line 31, where he is described as a Jew, engendered of giants. But see Kinsley: 'The suggestion that Damian is a *diabolus* perhaps owes something to the habit of presenting devils in a feathered costume (the standard dress of unfallen angels) in comic scenes in the mystery plays' (p. 344).

21 *Vane organis*: jugular veins, arteries

32–3 'The Jew was extremely ingenious and engendered by giants'. 'Jew', like 'Turk' earlier, is used simply to mean 'infidel'. In Genesis, the giants are the offspring of fallen angels and humans.

61 According to Lesley, he undertook to reach France ahead of the Scottish ambassadors who were leaving the same day, not Turkey.

65 *Dedalus*: Daedalus, the cunning craftsman, made wings for himself and his son Icarus to escape from Minos, King of Crete. Icarus, despite his father's warning, flew too near the sun which melted the wax in the wings so that he fell into the sea and was drowned.

66 *Menatair*: the Minotaur, a monster, part bull, part man, to accommodate whom Minos caused Daedalus to construct the Labyrinth.

67 *Martis blaksmith Vulcanus*: Vulcan (the Roman version of Hephaestus, the god of blacksmiths). The reference to Mars (who deceived Hephaestus with Aphrodite) is obscure.

68 *Saturnus*: as the Greek god, Kronos, chief of the Titans who preceded and were defeated by the Olympians; as the planet Saturn, traditionally a cold, infertile, malignant body.

23. THE TESTAMENT OF MAISTER ANDRO KENNEDY (C&M, B, M)
This goliardic satire belongs to the well-established tradition of the mock testament, which reaches back into late Latin (*Testamentum Porcelli* and *Testamentum Asini*), through the twelfth-century Archpoet's 'Meum est propositum in taberna mori', the anonymous French *Testament de Taste*

Vin, Villon's *Grand et Petit Testaments*, and *Colyn Blowbol's Testament* (with all of which Dunbar's poem has points of correspondence) and forward to Burns's 'Death and Dying Words of Poor Mailie' (for a full history of the mock testament as a literary form, see W.H. Rice, *The European Ancestry of Villon's Satirical Testaments*, New York, 1941). Dunbar probably took the form from Villon and his predecessors, and was to be followed in his use of it by Gavin Douglas (*King Hart*) and Sir David Lyndsay (*Testament and Complaynt of the Papyngo* and *Squyer Meldrum*). His mixture of Latin and English has been described as macaronic; strictly speaking, the true macaronic consists of attaching the endings of one language (for example, Latin) to the words of another (for example, Scots), as in William Drummond's *Polemo-Middinia*. But the general effect here is near enough for the term to be applicable; the dual language, which adds to the comic effect, reminds us that all the offices of the Church were then sung in Latin. Little is known of Andro Kennedy (no connection, as far as is known, of Walter Kennedy of no. 7, although M gives 'Walter Kennedy' in the opening line) but it has been assumed on slender evidence that he was a drunken court physician. That he was drunken seems clear but his profession is not confirmed.

2   'I come running when I am called'
3   *incuby*: St Augustine describes these creatures as 'silvans and fauns, commonly called incubi, [who] have often injured women, desiring and acting carnally with them' (*City of God*, trans. John Healey, 1962, bk xv, chap. xxiii).
6   'Where or whence I was born'
8   'that I am the devil incarnate'
9   'Since nothing is more certain than death'
11   'We know not when nor how'
12   *blind Allane wait of the mone*: a proverbial phrase
13   'I suffer in my breast'
15   Testators had to confirm their soundness in mind, even if (as here) sick in body.
17   'Now I write my testament'
19   'by means of almighty God'
21   'there to remain for ever more'
23   'to drink the good wine'
24   Sweet Cuthbert has not been identified.
25   'He is sweet for loving'
27   interjection: 'let him give me something to drink'
29   'because in the cellar, with the beer'
31   'naked but for my shirt'
35   'my inebriated body'
38   'in order that I may be buried there'
40   'on my face'
42   'but always inconstant'
44   'to my consort, Jacoba'
46   'I denied the true God'
48   'that pledge I always fulfilled'
49   *the best aucht*: on the death of a tenant in Carrick and Galloway

121

(which is Kennedy country), the landlord or head of the clan was entitled to claim his most valuable possession. James IV abolished this custom in 1490, but it probably persisted.

50 This line causes some difficulty. Kinsley reads *caupe* as a mature grazing beast, from the Gaelic *colpa*, which would normally be a clansman's most valuable possession. Bawcutt derives it from the Gaelic *colpa* for the tribute to the head of one's kin. It may be a composite pun on *colpa* and the Latin *caupo*, an innkeeper, the implication being that Kennedy's most valuable possession was his tavern-keeper.

51–2 'to the chief of my kin, but a curse on my head if I know who that is'

54 'but none of the others said this'

55 *sib as seve and riddill*: a proverbial saying, usually applied to those who claim kindred with those of higher position to whom they are not in fact related.

56 'that are grown in the same wood'

57–8 'all my comforts were only falsehoods one and all'

59 'all frauds and deceits', which testators usually disclaimed

60 *Sanct Antane*: the preceptory of St Antony, an order of religious knights, founded in 1435 by Sir Robert Logan of Restalrig at the south-west corner of St Antony's Wynd, Leith, and destroyed at the Reformation. 'The magistrates of Edinburgh appear to have regarded them with special favour. Among their civic dues, as noted in the Council Records, was the right of levying a quart of wine out of every tun brought into the town' (Daniel Wilson, *Memorials of Edinburgh in the Olden Time*, 1891, ii, 267).

61 'without payment'. William Gray has not been identified. Bawcutt (ed.) suggests that this might be an error for either Michael Gray, who was preceptor of St Anthony's in the 1440s, or William of Myrtoun, who held the post from 1489 to 1496.

63 'who never tells lies'

66 'I leave to the false friars'

68 'he distributed, he gave to the poor'

70 'they're liars, they do it for money'

72 'for their crooked dealings'

73 *Iok Fule*: Dunbar may have had a particular jester in mind; but the expression, Jock Fool, was proverbial for anyone stupid.

74 'I leave after the burial of my body'

78 'although he shows a good appearance' (put a good face on it?)

80 'pretending to be a fool'

81 *Johne Clerk*: identity not known.

82 'I give and bequeath cordially'

84 'he is the cause of my death'

86 'many marvel at me'

88 The point of this jibe ('writing "dentes" [teeth] without the d') is now obscure.

89 'My residuary estate'

91 'with guardianship of the children' (since he is called 'Maister',

Kennedy would be at least in minor orders and therefore theoretically celibate)

94 'I make arrangements for the funeral'
96 'not in the usual way'
97 'On the day of my burial'
99 'and two peasants from the country'
102 'as I've been accustomed to do myself'
104 A ribald quotation from Psalm 102, 9: 'For I have eaten ashes like bread: and mingled my drinks with weeping'.
106 A quotation from the Mass for the Dead: 'that day, the day of wrath'
108 'as is usually done'
110 'carrying a bunch of hay [sign of an alehouse] before me'
112 'four narrow-necked flagons'
114 'beside me, in the same way as a Cross'
116 See Psalm 119, 73, 'Thou has made me from dust'; but the quotation is more closely related to the burial service in the *Sarum Missal*: 'De terra plasmasti me et carne induisti me redemptor meus domine resuscita me in novissimo die'.

24. THE DREGY OF DUNBAR (B, M)

Here again Dunbar parodies the liturgy, a common exercise among medieval poets. It was the king's custom to make a yearly retreat, usually at Lent and Advent, at the Friary of the Observant Franciscans which he had established at Stirling, and to spend his time there in prayer, fasting and penance for the welfare of his soul. The courtiers who accompanied him would perforce share the same austerities. Dunbar, in this brilliant parody of the Office of the Dead, condoles with the king and his companions. 'Dregy', or 'dirge' is a corruption of the opening word of the antiphon at matins ('Dirige, Deus meus, in conspectu tuo viam meam') and, after an introduction, Dunbar goes on to rewrite other parts of the office. This consisted of vespers, matins (with three nocturns, each with three psalms and three *lectios* or lessons), and lauds. Dunbar provides three *lectios*, in octosyllabic couplets, with responses in the form of French triolets. The final fourteen lines are a parody of phrases from the Lord's Prayer and from vespers of the Office of the Dead. For an excellent analysis of the parodic virtuosity of the poem, see Bawcutt, pp. 194–203. The wit, apart from the pure verbal dexterity, consists in the reversal of values: James and his companions, who are engaged in godly pursuits, are pictured as suffering the torments of hell; Dunbar and his cronies, in the guise of a celestial choir, describe the unbridled eating and drinking in Edinburgh as the joys of Paradise – as Scott has pointed out, 'sensuality is life, and spirituality is death' (p. 220).

15 *but cumpany*: without the company
45 The patriarchs consisted of Abraham, Isaac, Jacob and Jacob's twelve sons.
59 *Sanct Jeill*: St Giles or Aegidius, the patron saint of beggars, to whom the High Church in Edinburgh is dedicated.
66 *sterris sevin*: normally the Pleiades; here, Bawcutt (ed.) suggests that it indicates the seven planets, each of which, in medieval

astronomy, revolved one of the spheres which encircled the earth. God and his saints dwelt beyond the planetary spheres and the Primum Mobile.

97–111   Most of this section is lifted direct from either the Lord's Prayer or from the Office of the Dead (vespers), apart from the addition or substitution of either 'Strivilling' or 'Edinburgi' in appropriate places, and the significant addition of the word 'corpora' to line 102, viz: 'and lead us not into the temptations of Stirling; but deliver us from that evil. The peace of Edinburgh give them, O Lord, and let its light shine upon them. From the wretched gates of Stirling, Lord, lead forth their souls and bodies. I know that I shall taste steadfastly the wine of Edinburgh in the town of the living. May they rest in Edinburgh, Amen. God, who deigns to free the just and humble in heart from all their tribulations, liberate your servants who dwell in the town of Stirling from the pains and sorrows of that place and lead them to the joys of Edinburgh, that Stirling may rest in peace. Amen.'

25.   TO THE MERCHANTIS OF EDINBURGH (R)
This poem provides a salutory corrective to the traditional view of the golden age of James IV. The first consideration in the building of medieval Edinburgh (as in so many other cities of the period) was security. A nation as frequently invaded as lowland Scotland put ease of defence before other qualities; and Edinburgh was well placed in this respect, situated on a narrow spine of rock running down from the volcanic outcrop on which the Castle was built to the Abbey of Holyrood (to which James IV added a palace for the reception of his queen) at the foot. To the north side of this spine lay the Nor'loch, now drained, and beyond it the Firth of Forth. To the south, whence attack most commonly came, the ground fell away to open country and the city was walled; new walls had been built in 1450. In consequence, all urban activity, commercial, residential, political, religious, was confined within a small, cramped space and in a density of population almost unimaginable today. The citizens, even the most nobly born, unable to spread out, built up towards the sky in high tenements which virtually shut out light and air from the main street and the narrow wynds which ran between them. The tenements, as in so many medieval cities, were built at right angles to the main street, the gable end presenting a suitable shelter for encrustations of shops and stalls which also cluttered the outside of St Giles' Cathedral. There was no plumbing, sewage or rubbish disposal. The stanza which Dunbar uses to describe the resulting squalor is a collateral ancestor of the Burns stanza; and Dunbar demonstrates early, as Ramsay and Burns were to do much later, how admirably its metrical arrangement lends itself to the rhythms of colloquial speech.

15   This was probably not Edinburgh's most distinguished school, the Royal High School, which the Town Council Register refers to as being fostered in 1519 (there are records of a building being authorised for it in 1554). It may have been a school attached to St Giles' Cathedral or to the Old Tolbooth.

17   *foirstair*: an outside stair, leading up to the main floor of the
     building.
24   *Trone*: the tron, the public weighing machine, usually set up in or
     near the market place, and also used as a pillory.
29   *tone*: tune. Of the two tunes recorded in line 30, 'Into Joun' has
     disappeared. 'Now the day dawis' has a long popular pedigree
     (though this is one of its earliest sightings) and was eventually
     turned into one of the *Gude and Godlie Ballatis* after the Reformation.
31   *Sanct Cloun*: identified by Kinsley with a St Cluanus, a sixth-century
     Irish Abbot, apparently identified with eating and drinking. The
     implication is that skilled craftsmen, who could do better work, are
     forced to serve the trade of St Cluanus.
36   Dunbar gives more attention to the tailors and cobblers in no. 31.
38   *styll*: here, not a style but a steep lane, on the north side of St Giles.
     See Bawcutt, p. 406.
71–2 An early attack on the evils of capitalism.
77   Reidpeth has left a gap here in his manuscript. Various solutions
     have been proposed. Small's suggestion of 'win bak to' is
     convincing.

26.   THE TWA CUMMERIS (B, M; there is also a text in the Aberdeen
      Minute Book of Seisins)
Pinkerton in 1786 was the earliest critic to point out the resemblance of
this poem to Dutch interior painting: since then, many have done so, and
Simpson Ross provides a list of paintings which might have served as
models, had they not all been painted well over a hundred years too late.
Dunbar has combined standard ridicule of the commands of the church
with an element of the *chanson de mal mariée* tradition and produced a
light-hearted satirical masterpiece. The irony of the poem is made clear
in the first line, with the words 'Rycht airlie on Ask Weddinsday'; Ash
Wednesday is the first of the forty days of Lent, and the two women have
presumably endured its rigours for as long as six hours (and indeed are
probably still suffering from a Shrove Tuesday hangover) before they
start to complain. Scott reads it as a satire on a male-dominated, patriar-
chal society (p. 66).
2   *cumeris*: originally a godmother (cp. the French *commère*), but more
      often used for intimate female friends or neighbours.
12   *nigertnes*: normally, niggardliness; M's *migarnes* ('meagreness',
      'thinness') is more likely.
14   *mavasy*: malmsey. 'this strong, sweet wine originally from the
      Morea in Greece and then made in Spain and the Azores and
      Canaries was imported into Scotland from the staple at
      Middleburgh in Holland' (Simpson Ross, p. 180).
30   M: *That lentrune swld nocht mak thame lene.*

27.   THE TRETIS OF THE TUA MARIIT WEMEN AND THE WEDO (M. An
      incomplete text (line 104 to the end), which varies considerably
      from M, is found in C&M.)
In this poem Dunbar carries to a high point of virtuosity his custom of

125

taking conventional medieval forms (most of them, in French literature of the period, looking mechanical and worn out by this time) and using them inventively and subversively. Like no. 18, it opens as a traditional *chanson d'aventure*, the account of the eavesdropping poet, then moves on from this to embrace the *chanson de mal mariée* tradition, the complaint of the unhappily married woman. There is an element of the conventional *débat*, in which a question is posed and debated, and it finishes with the traditional *demande d'amour* from the poet to his audience, which could open a fresh debate. The setting is the traditional idealised garden, inherited from the *Roman de la Rose*, but the matter is not at all romantic and courtly, and introduces yet another tradition, a kind of third-party flyting of the women with their absent husbands. Descriptions of it as a satire on women or comparisons with Chaucer's Wife of Bath are alike unsatisfactory. C.S. Lewis got nearest the mark when he described it as a practical joke: 'That is the point of the idyllic opening which contains not the slightest hint of what is to follow. You are to picture the audience at its first recitation, and especially the ladies in that audience... settling themselves to enjoy a serious allegory or a serious romance, full of the "honour of love", and then to imagine with what shattering detonation the main body of the poem burst upon them. The almost unparalleled grossness of the things the three women say is not there for the sake of character drawing. The fun lies in its sheer preposterousness and in the virtuosity with which the poet goes on piling audacity on audacity – and on the ludicrous contrast between this and their appearance' (p. 94). It also lies in the contrast between the *amour courtois* setting and the realities of medieval marriage in which dowries and lands carry more weight than *amour* of any kind (and through which alone women could achieve the only kind of independence open to them, as the widow proves). Part of the joke, as Lewis points out, is the contrast between the standard romance descriptions of the ladies ('the semely', 'the plesand', 'this amyable', 'thir ryall rosis') and their gross behaviour, which is reinforced by the fact that, though they are initially described as ladies of the court, it soon becomes clear that they are from a very much lower social order. Though many of the traditions embodied in the poem are of French descent, Dunbar has chosen to write it in the old stressed alliterative line associated both with the flyting and burlesque traditions and with sophisticated court poetry, and involving the use of vocabulary not found elsewhere in his work. The apparent anti-feminist element is slightly misleading, since Dunbar appears to have some sympathy with the wives in their marital predicaments, however lewd and hypocritical their behaviour (see, for example, lines 211–16), and what at first sight seems to be typical clerical misogyny actually has a subtle feminist subtext.

1   Midsummer Eve was probably chosen for the setting deliberately, since it was associated with folk and fertility rituals, hence love-making.

4   Hawthorn, like the rowan, was believed to have magic and protective powers.

12   *hautand*: normally haughty, elevated – but also an early indication

that the ladies are not so very elegant, since they are drinking and talking loudly.

24   *mantillis grein*: the significance of colours was extremely important in the Middle Ages. Green was the colour of amorous passion. Cp. the anonymous fifteenth-century French song: 'Il te fauldra de vert vestir, / C'est la livrée aux amoureux'.

36   *wlonkes*: ladies, a term normally used only in alliterative verse.

58   Huizinga (p. 105) quotes Pierre Col who, in his defence of the *Roman de la Rose* (*c*.1400), writes that Nature does not wish that a woman should be content with one single man.

60   *bernis*: men, fellows (originally from the OE *beorn*, a warrior); another alliterative poetic term.

60–3 Dunbar would have found a model for his libertarian society in Ovid's *Metamorphoses*, x, 320ff. (though this is more a justification of incest) but also in Lydgate's *Floure of Curtesye*.

85   *A forky fure*: no such word as 'forky' is known outside this poem. 'Fure' can mean a fellow, a furrow or to fare, go. Kinsley suggests two possible emendations: 'Ay forthy [that is, forward, enterprising] to fure' or 'Ay forthy in fure', neither very convincing. 'A forky fellow' fits better, and the sense of the adjective has to be deduced from the context.

101 *Mahowne*: the principal heretic, that is, the devil.

106 *schowis one me*: this is Kinsley's emendation and preferable to M's reading, 'Chowis me'.

112 *Belȝebub*: god of flies, Satan.

123–4 'Contriving and calculating a thousand ways, how he can catch me by a trick at a tryst with someone else'

139 *engranyt*: ingraining was the most expensive dyeing process, usually associated with a high-quality dye such as cochineal.

142 *Johne Blunt*: stupid John.

159–61 *That of ȝour toungis ȝe be traist... ther is no spy neir*: the exhortation to discretion reminds the reader of the poet lurking in the hedge.

168 *hur maister*: a frequenter of whores, rather than a brothel keeper. Pitscottie records that 'the bischope of Murray quhilk ever was ane hure maister all his dayis... wald not put away his hure' (*Historie and Cronicles of Scotland*, ed. A.J.G. Mackay, STS, 1899–1911, ii, 141).

176 'It's a waste of time giving that tired snail a rest.'

198 *Bot he nought ane is, bot nane*: 'but he isn't one, not one'. The repetition is for added emphasis.

210 *freke*: man (a poetic term common in alliterative verse)

231 *put thole*: endure a hard push

234 'She would not be shifted a step by his thrust'

238 'I bet that girl wouldn't joke about my happiness'.

244 *pertlyar*: more impudently (another slap at the unseemliness of their behaviour and loud speech)

245 Dunbar has constructed the widow's speech as a satire on the writing of a sermon, as outlined in medieval treatises on the art of preaching, starting with the invocation (lines 247–50), continuing

with the *thema* or main text (line 251), and the *exampla* (line 270).
See A.C. Spearing, *Criticism and Medieval Poetry*, 1964, pp. 72–7.

252   *schene in my schrowd*: a stock alliterative phrase ('fair in my gown')
275   *krych*: M reads *claw*, C&M reads *keyth* (not otherwise known);
      Kinsley (p. 270) adopted the emendation *krych* (a variant of 'critch',
      'cratch', to scratch), which better maintains the alliterative pattern.
301   'But I so often reminded him of it, which angered his heart'
306   *knew*: it is, probably deliberately, unclear whether the word is used
      here biblically or not.
331   This image is clearly inspired by medieval stories and illustrations
      of the courtesan Campaspe riding Aristotle, saddled and bridled.
      Dunbar could have seen bas-reliefs of this legend on the cathedrals
      at Caen and Rouen during his travels in France (see Mâle, pp.
      334–5).
348–50   Having pictured her husband as the beast of burden which she
      rides, she now speaks of herself as having been curbed by a bridle
      till she breaks the reins in pieces. In line 354, he is again being
      ridden on a tight rein.
362   Because Lombardy was the centre of the medieval banking indus-
      try, bankers were often pejoratively referred to as 'Lombards'.
421   Churches were so frequently used as meeting or trysting places by
      lovers in the fifteenth century that no particular obliquity attaches
      to the widow for this (cp. also l. 81). Even the virtuous fourteenth-
      century French poet Christine de Pisan makes a lover say, 'Se
      souvent vais ou moustier, / C'est tout pour voir la belle / Fresche
      comme rose nouvelle' [If I often go to church, it's just to see the fair
      lady, fresh as a newly-opened rose].
424   Another subtle hint of the privileged position the widow had
      achieved. In medieval churches, most of the congregation stood;
      she has got herself a seat.
476–85   In middle Scots, unlike English, the third person plural verb
      ends in -s or -is. The whole of this passage indicates that the high-
      born widow is no more than a whore, albeit one with the proverbial
      heart of gold (see lines 499–501).
502   *Sabot*: M has the nonsensical 'sall not'; C&M's 'Sabot' (from
      'Sabaoth', 'Dominus Sabaoth' Lord of hosts) is clearly right.
503   *lassis*: lasses, in the sense of schoolgirls, green girls
504   Legends, in the sense that the word is used here, were normally
      written of saints' lives and read aloud as part of the official teaching
      of the church. The use of the word by the widow to describe her
      own life therefore verges on blasphemy.

28.   QUHAT IS THIS LYFE (M)

Bawcutt (pp. 145–6) suggests that this short lyric may be a stanza
excerpted from a longer work, now lost. Any poem on this theme, chal-
lenges comparison with Chaucer's

What is this world? what asketh men to have?
Now with his love, now in his colde grave

Allone, withouten any compaignye.

If, in this short fragment, Dunbar does not quite attain Chaucer's concentrated wonder at the mystery of life and death, it must be remembered that he was a priest, and saw that mystery first and foremost in eschatological terms. His lyricism is certainly equal to Chaucer's.

3   The conventional medieval image of the wheel of fortune, on which men rise and fall, does not quite fit here, unless the implication is that the fall, when the wheel turns, causes the victim to seek remedy from God.

6–7   That is, the short torment of life is a small price to pay for those who attain bliss, but the joys of a sinful life will be a short consolation for the eternal pains of hell.

29.   SWEIT ROIS OF VERTEW (M)

The love lyric barely existed in Scotland before Dunbar, though he could have found exemplars in England and France. Here, the form seems to have sprung, fully developed, from his brain. Nothing written before in Scotland is comparable, either to its tenderness or to its perfection of form, and it is necessary to wait for the lyrics of Alexander Scott and Mark Alexander Boyd for anything to equal it. It was probably written to be sung, but no setting has been discovered.

3   *bontie*: this, whether in Scots, English, French or Italian, had a stronger meaning in the Middle Ages than simple 'goodness'; there should also be a suggestion of spiritual grace, of generosity. Cp. Ariosto's 'O gran bontà de' cavallieri antichi!'.

8   The mention of white and red flowers suggests that the poem might have been written for the young Tudor queen (which would also explain her 'mercilessness'); but it is unwise to build too much on a standard phrase.

10   *rew*: the herb rue, Ophelia's 'herb of grace'. Dunbar is credited by the OED as the first person to make a punning connection between the herb rue, and rue in the sense of pity.

30.   INCONSTANCY OF LUVE (B)

The main cleverness of this poem consists in the structure which uses a version of the tail-rhyme stanza which would eventually descend to Burns, and produces twenty-four lines on two rhymes only. It is love itself, not any particular lady, who is attacked here. A more cynical and pessimistic piece than no. 29, it lingers in the mind not only for the ingenuity of its construction but for the unforgettable closing image.

31.   FASTERNIS EVIN IN HELL

The Dance: B, M, R
The Sowtar and Tail3ouris War: B, M, A
The Amendis: B, M

In B, the three following poems are printed one after the other, with the clear intention that they should be regarded as an integral sequence. In M, despite some disarrangement of the text, the unity of the first two at least is emphasised. I have followed Kinsley's solution of printing them as a trio, each of which follows on logically from the other, and have also borrowed his title for the sequence. This is one of the few occasions when it seems possible to give a date to any of Dunbar's poems; during the years when we know Dunbar to have been active, Fastern's Eve (Shrove Tuesday) fell on 16 February in 1507. See, however, Bawcutt (ed.), 2, 384.

The portrayal of the cardinal virtues and vices in medieval churches and cathedrals, and indeed in morality plays, was common, and the depiction of the dance of the seven deadly sins, even more so. There were different versions of the list, but Dunbar, in his poem, and in the order in which they appear, follows St Gregory. As a priest, Dunbar would have been familiar with manuals which dealt with the subject and also with the appearance of the sins in *Piers Plowman*, Lydgate's *Dance of Death*, Gower's *Confessio Amantis*, and Chaucer's *Parson's Tale*. What is peculiar to Dunbar is the eldritch relish with which he describes them. C. S. Lewis points out that laughing at the devil was a braver thing to do when men believed in him: 'notice... that we are laughing at torture. The grotesque figures skip through fire, jag each other with knives, and are constantly spewing out molten gold... Dunbar and his contemporaries seriously believed that such entertainment awaited in the next world those who had practised (without repentance) the seven deadly sins in this' (p. 95). Kinsley, who in his edition provides useful examples of contemporary representations of the Sins (as does Simpson Ross), observes that though representations of the sins were common in didactic literature, painting and carving, Dunbar has subverted the usual portrayal: 'to present this pageant in hell before an audience of devils, and to throw it, not into the formal allegorical procession of the painters and poets, but into the wild swirl of a dance, seem to be original notions of Dunbar's' (p. 336).

The tournament of the tailors and cobblers springs also from traditional roots, but not religious ones. Both tradesmen were routine targets of satire, and the description of both (for example, lousy and dishonest tailors and oily cobblers) can be paralleled in other poems, for example in another poem in the Bannatyne MS, 'The flyting betuix the sowtar and the tailȝor', though the anonymous author of this might well have drawn on Dunbar (see also line 121, note, below). A better parallel is with the combat between two burghers of Valenciennes before Duke Philip of Burgundy in 1455, described by George Chastellain (Huizinga, p. 89). In this contest, the loser was hanged. A mock tournament of this kind could only be portrayed towards the end of the Middle Ages when the chivalric ideals which had upheld the concepts of knighthood and the traditional tournament had all but broken down, and the tournament described here has many parallels, as has been noted by other critics, with Scottish brawl poems such as 'Christis Kirk on the Grene' and 'Peblis to the Play', which have their roots in folk tradition.

Dunbar sets all three parts within the conventional dream framework: one dream contains the 'Dance' and the 'Tournament', the latter causing him to laugh so much that he wakes himself up. The 'Amendis' is set in a separate dream.

The Dance of the Sevin Deidly Synnis

17   *hair*: all texts have *bair*; all editions except Bawcutt amend this to *hair*, which makes better sense with the 'bonet' reference. The image of Pride, with 'bonet on syd', recalls the lecherous husband in no. 27 (line 180).

18   *wastie wanis*: ruined dwellings, presumably through extravagance.

30   *Blak Belly and Bawsy Broun*: presumably two devils. Kinsley points out references to two devil-torturers in Roull's *Cursing* (c.1500, Maitland Folio MS), called Brownie and Bellie Basie (p. 337).

49–54 The followers of Envy vividly recall Dunbar's complaints in other poems, for example, no. 16, lines 41–5.

64–6 An interesting modern variant of this torture is found in Lawrence Norfolk's *Lemprière's Dictionary*, where a girl is murdered by having molten gold poured down her throat.

77   *Thay* in this line presumably refers to the devils.

81   *Ydilnes*: M's *Lythenes* (lightness, wantonness) would preserve the alliteration better.

86–7 It has been suggested that these lines describe the early signs of leprosy, which was believed in the Middle Ages to be sexually transmitted – hence presumably the reason why Henryson afflicted his Cresseid with it.

104–5 It is not clear why minstrels (except for the murderer) are excluded, unless because music would have mitigated the pains of hell. This adds to the irony of the following stanza: the *correnoch* is clearly not music.

108   *breif of richt*: a legal process by which a claim could be established to heritable property. The property to which the murderous minstrel could lay claim by virtue of his crime is hell.

110   *Makfadȝane*: a stock Highland name.

113–20 This is standard Lowland contempt for Highlanders (cp. Dunbar's taunts to the Gaelic-speaking Kennedy in no. 7).

The Sowtar and Tailȝouris War

121   Mock tournaments between servants or tradesmen were recorded at the courts of James V and Mary, and may have been held by James IV also, though no record has survived.

136   Tailors' habit of stealing bits of cloth is frequently referred to in contemporary literature.

137   *greik sie*: the tideless Mediterranean, which never ebbs or flows

147   *mast*: presumably a ship's mast

149   *curage*: M's reading. B: *hairt*

158   The defender in a tournament always came from the west end of the lists; the challenger came from the east.

164   *Sanct Girnega*: Roull's *Cursing* (Maitland Folio MS) has Girnega as a devil together with Gog and Magog.

201–7 *he* is the Devil.

The Amendis

The Maitland text has the colophon, 'Quod dumbar quhone he drank to

the Dekynnis for amendis to the bodeis of thair craftis'. This last
poem in the sequence, which is outside the original trance or
dream, was presumably added to appease the tailors and cobblers,
notwithstanding its penultimate line.

32. ALL ERDLY JOY RETURNIS IN PANE (B, M)
After Shrove Tuesday, Ash Wednesday. This song for the first morning
of Lent, written in the same stanza as the preceding poem but in a very
different spirit, sounds a properly didactic and moral note. Simpson Ross
points out that there are exactly forty lines in the poem, the same number
as the days in Lent, and that the imagery of the destruction of fruit and
grain offers a parallel in Nature to the passion and death of Christ.

4   This refrain can be found in varying forms in the work of many late
     medieval poets. Note particularly Henryson's 'of erdly joy ay
     sorow is the end' ('The Prais of Aige', line 26) and Douglas's
     'Temporal ioy endis wyth wo and pane' (*Eneados*, iv, 221).
11   *flowring grane*: that this is intended as an image of Christ, devoured
     by death, is supported by no. 34, line 72, 'That baire the gloryus
     grayne'.

33. LAMENT FOR THE MAKARIS (C&M, B, M)
C&M is the only text to have the colophon 'quod Dunbar quhen he wes
sek', but, as the only text known to have been produced in his lifetime
and probably in Edinburgh, it carries authority. This is probably the most
famous of Dunbar's poems and certainly the most often quoted. The
danse macabre, the procession of all kinds of mortals towards death, was
nothing new in medieval literature, and examples, written and pictorial,
abound (see Kinsley, pp. 352–3). Huizinga points out that in the fifteenth
century, popular woodcuts of the dance, for example, those of the
Parisian printer, Guyot Marchant (1485), were added to carvings and
paintings. If Dunbar had not come across one elsewhere, he could have
seen a good example carved on the walls of Roslin Chapel, near
Edinburgh, probably dating from the fifteenth century. As usual,
however, he has given a new twist to a conventional form, first by starting
(and finishing) with a purely personal stanza which touches the core of
the human condition, and then by turning the usual impersonal proces-
sion of types into a very personal celebration of named fellow-poets,
many of them probably known to him. The refrain, already used by
Lydgate, would of course have been familiar to him as a priest from the
Office of the Dead (third nocturn, seventh lesson): 'Peccantem me
quotidie et non me poenitentem timor mortis conturbat me: Quia in
inferno nulla est redemptio, miserere mei, Deus, et salva me'. Kinsley
points out that, though Dunbar would certainly have died and been
buried as a priest, he places himself here with the poets, his brethren.
     The terminal date for composition must be 1508, when C&M printed
it; but line 86 suggests a date in late 1505 (see note below). The poem is
untitled in all sources. This well-known title originated in the eighteenth
century.
4   'The fear of death terrifies me'. The Latin words originate in the

Office of the Dead.

21–2 C&M's readings are less satisfactory, so B has been adopted for these lines.

37 *Art magicianis*: those who practise the art of magic

50 Geoffrey Chaucer (*c*.1343–1400) rightly heads the list of poets as the eldest of them and the greatest.

51 *The monk of Bery*: John Lydgate (1370?–1451?) was a monk in the monastery of Bury, Bury St Edmunds. John Gower (1330?–1408) wrote mainly in Latin and French; his best-known English work, *Confessio Amantis*, was published by Caxton in 1483.

53 *Syr Hew of Eglintoun*: Dunbar starts here his roll-call of the Scots poets. Sir Hew has been identified by Kinsley as Sir Hugh Eglintoun of that Ilk (d. 1377), brother-in-law of Robert II and not otherwise known as a poet; the possibility that there may have been another Hew Eglintoun who was a poet cannot be dismissed (for further notes on the Scots poets, see Baxter, pp. 229–34).

54 *Heryot and Wyntoun*: Heryot is unknown. Andrew of Wyntoun (1350?–1422?), prior of St Serf's Priory, Loch Leven, wrote the metrical *Oryginale Chronykil of Scotland*.

58 *Maister Johne Clerk and James Afflek*: a number of poems in B are attributed to 'Clerk', but clearly more than one Clerk was a poet (see line 65 below). It has been suggested that James Afflek (or Auchinleck) is the author of *The Quare of Jelusy*, preserved in the same manuscript as *The Kingis Quair*, which has a colophon deciphered by David Laing as 'quod Auchen...'. He may also be the James Auchlek who graduated (like Dunbar) at St Andrews in 1471, was secretary to the Earl of Ross and Precentor of Caithness in 1494 and died in September 1497.

61 *Holland and Barbour*: Sir Richard Holland (fl.1450), author of *The Buke of the Howlat*. John Barbour (1316?–95), archdeacon of Aberdeen, wrote *Brus*, the famous celebration of the War of Independence.

63 *Schir Mungo Lokert of the Le*: the Lockharts of the Lee were an old Lanarkshire family, but nothing is known of this particular member.

65 *Clerk of Tranent* has not been identified. *The Anteris of Gawane* has not survived.

67 *Schir Gilbert Hay*: Sir Gilbert de la Hay (fl. *c*.1405–60), knighted at Senlis 1428, chamberlain to Charles VII of France and later a priest in the household of the Earl of Caithness. He translated (in prose) *The Buke of the Law of Armys*, *The Buke of Knychthede* and *The Buke of the Governaunce of Princis* and also made a verse translation of the *Roman d'Alixandre*.

69 *Blind Hary*: author of *Wallace*. M.P. McDiarmid's edition of the poem (STS, I, xxvi–lx) has much enlarged previous biographical information about him and shows both that he was probably not blind when he wrote the poem and that he appears as a recipient of grants in *LHTA* between 1490 and 1492, in which case Dunbar may well have known him. He also suggests that he may have been

the author of the alliterative tales, *Rauf Coilȝear* and *Golagros and Gawane*. Nothing is known of Sandy Traill.

71 *Patrik Johnestoun*: according to Kinsley, official receiver of revenues from West Lothian crown lands paid to him for plays before the king, 1476–7; he died *c.*1494–5. *The Thre Deid Pollis* is attributed to him in B, though M gives it to Henryson.

73 *Merseir*: B contains a number of poems attributed to Mersar, but nothing more is known of him than this, except that Lyndsay refers to him in his *Testament of the Papyngo* (line 19).

77–8 One of these two Roulls was presumably the author of the spirited *The Cursing of Sr Johine Rowlis upoun the steilaris of his fowlis* (B, ii, 277) and probably the Rowle referred to by Lyndsay in *The Testament of the Papyngo* (line 19), but which there is no way of knowing.

82 *Maister Robert Henrisoun*: schoolmaster in Dunfermline, presumably in the Abbey School, and author of *The Testament of Cresseid* and *The Morall Fabillis of Esope the Phrygian*. He was unarguably the greatest of Dunbar's contemporaries.

83 *Schir Johne the Ros*: Dunbar's second in his flyting with Kennedy, but none of his writing has survived. It has been suggested that he is either Sir John the Ross of Montgrenan, Ayrshire (d.1494), or Sir John Ross of Halkhead, sheriff of West Lothian (dead by 1502).

86 *Stobo*: Kinsley identifies him as John Reid, 'alias Stobo', rector of Kirkcrist in Kirkcudbright, secretary to James II, James III and James IV, noted in the Exchequer Rolls as sick in May 1505 in *LHTA* and as dead in July. *Quintyne Schaw*: M attributes to him a poem beginning 'Suppois the courte ȝow cheir and tretis' (I, 384–5); he apparently received a pension of £10 in 1504.

89 *Gud Maister Walter Kennedy*: Dunbar's opponent in the flyting (no. 7). Some of his poems survive in B and M and he is mentioned respectfully by Lyndsay (*Testament of the Papyngo*) and Douglas (*Palice of Honour*). Dunbar says that he lies 'in poynt of dede', but he may have recovered.

34. ANE BALLAT OF OUR LADY (A)

Dunbar is often described as an 'aureate' poet and here we have an example of his work at its most aureate. This is, it has been suggested, the style most natural to him. However, no other poem of his which has survived is so elaborately decorated, though many other poems contain aureate phrases. Nor, had the works of his contemporaries all survived, might this have been picked out as exceptionally gilded; it was not of Dunbar but of his flyting rival, Kennedy, that Lyndsay was to write 'Or quho can now the workis cuntrafait / Off Kennedie, with termis aureait?'. In other poems, Dunbar has used aureation occasionally, as in no. 2, to mark a particularly auspicious or important state occasion or make a point. Here, exceptionally, he has employed the full battery of his aureate vocabulary and the ecstatic intricacies of his metrical skill to celebrate the Queen of Heaven, a context in which aureate diction was conventionally used. He has even contrived to combine alliteration with his complicated rhyme scheme. The refrain is the first line of the 'Hail Mary' (Luke, i, 28).

1   In many paintings the Virgin is shown with a star (her symbol) pinned to her robe.

14   *Alphais habitakle*: the Virgin is the habitation of God, who is 'alpha et omega'.

29   As Eve was shown in medieval art to be vanquished by the serpent, so Mary is depicted overcoming a dragon or devil.

43   *daseyne*: daisy, literally 'the eyes of day'

47   *ga betweyne*: the traditional role of the Virgin, as intercessor between God and man.

72   *gloryus grayne*: cp. the image in no. 32, line 11, 'devoring fruct and flowring grane'.

73   *wall*: well, an image of the chastity of Mary (Kinsley). Bawcutt justifies 'wall'.

35.   OF THE NATIVITIE OF CHRIST (B)
This Christmas carol, one of Dunbar's finest religious poems, shows him still in aureate mood but less so than in no. 34. Here, what strikes the reader is less the metrical and verbal ingenuity than the exultant joy and lyricism. Dunbar is celebrating the medieval feast of the Nativity, still closely linked in its imagery to the pagan fertility festivals out of which it developed. The metre suggests that it may have been intended to be sung, though no setting has survived; it is, as C. S. Lewis wrote, 'the most lyrical of all English poems – that is, the hardest of all English poems simply to *read*, the hardest not to sing' (p. 95).

1   The second line is a translation of the first.

8   'unto us a boy is born' (Isaiah, ix, 6).

49   In the medieval vision of the universe, which postulated a series of concentric circles radiating out from the Earth, Heaven was the outermost circle.

36.   ON THE RESURRECTION OF CHRIST (B)
This hymn for the resurrection must unarguably be one of the greatest of Dunbar's poems. Unlike no. 35, it does not demand to be sung: it is a cry of triumph, of deep conviction, grandeur and dignity. None of the images is original, all can be paralleled in countless other poems or in visual art; what is unique is the majestic expression. The theme of the harrowing of hell by Christ in the period between his death and resurrection appeared first in the apocryphal gospel of Nicodemus.

8   'The Lord has risen from the grave.'

FyfieldBooks

Two millennia of essential classics
The extensive FyfieldBooks list includes

Djuna Barnes *The Book of Repulsive Women and other poems*
edited by Rebecca Loncraine

Elizabeth Barrett Browning *Selected Poems* edited by Malcolm Hicks

Charles Baudelaire *Complete Poems in French and English*
translated by Walter Martin

The Brontë Sisters *Selected Poems*
edited by Stevie Davies

Lewis Carroll *Selected Poems*
edited by Keith Silver

Thomas Chatterton *Selected Poems*
edited by Grevel Lindop

John Clare *By Himself*
edited by Eric Robinson and David Powell

Samuel Taylor Coleridge *Selected Poetry* edited by William Empson and David Pirie

John Donne *Selected Letters*
edited by P.M. Oliver

Oliver Goldsmith *Selected Writings*
edited by John Lucas

Victor Hugo *Selected Poetry in French and English*
translated by Steven Monte

Wyndham Lewis *Collected Poems and Plays* edited by Alan Munton

Charles Lamb *Selected Writings*
edited by J.E. Morpurgo

Ben Jonson *Epigrams and The Forest*
edited by Richard Dutton

Giacomo Leopardi *The Canti with a selection of his prose*
translated by J.G. Nichols

Andrew Marvell *Selected Poems*
edited by Bill Hutchings

Charlotte Mew *Collected Poems and Selected Prose*
edited by Val Warner

Michelangelo *Sonnets*
translated by Elizabeth Jennings, introduction by Michael Ayrton

William Morris *Selected Poems*
edited by Peter Faulkner

Ovid *Amores*
translated by Tom Bishop

Edgar Allan Poe *Poems and Essays on Poetry*
edited by C.H. Sisson

Restoration Bawdy
edited by John Adlard

Rainer Maria Rilke *Sonnets to Orpheus and Letters to a Young Poet*
translated by Stephen Cohn

Christina Rossetti *Selected Poems*
edited by C.H. Sisson

Sir Walter Scott *Selected Poems*
edited by James Reed

Sir Philip Sidney *Selected Writings*
edited by Richard Dutton

Henry Howard, Earl of Surrey *Selected Poems*
edited by Dennis Keene

Algernon Charles Swinburne *Selected Poems*
edited by L.M. Findlay

Oscar Wilde *Selected Poems*
edited by Malcolm Hicks

Sir Thomas Wyatt *Selected Poems*
edited by Hardiman Scott

For more information, including a full list of FyfieldBooks and a contents list for each title, and details of how to order the books in the UK, visit the Fyfield website at www.fyfieldbooks.co.uk or email info@fyfieldbooks.co.uk. For information about FyfieldBooks available in the United States and Canada, visit the Routledge website at www.routledge-ny.com.